The World Famous
IVERSON
Movie Ranch

Real Land of Make Believe

Superman (1948)
Kirk Alyn

Hopalong Cassidy
William Boyd and Young Friends

Vultura
Lorna Gray

The World Famous
IVERSON
Movie Ranch

Real Land of Make Believe

by
Jerry L. Schneider

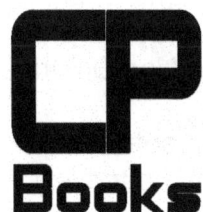

CP
Books

A CP Book
First Edition
October 2018

Published by
CP Books

For a list of our books, please visit our web site at
www.CPEntBooks.com

ISBN: 978-0999367247 (Special Edition softcover)
ISBN: 978-0999367254 (Regular Edition softcover)

The World Famous

IVERSON

Movie Ranch

Real Land of Make Believe

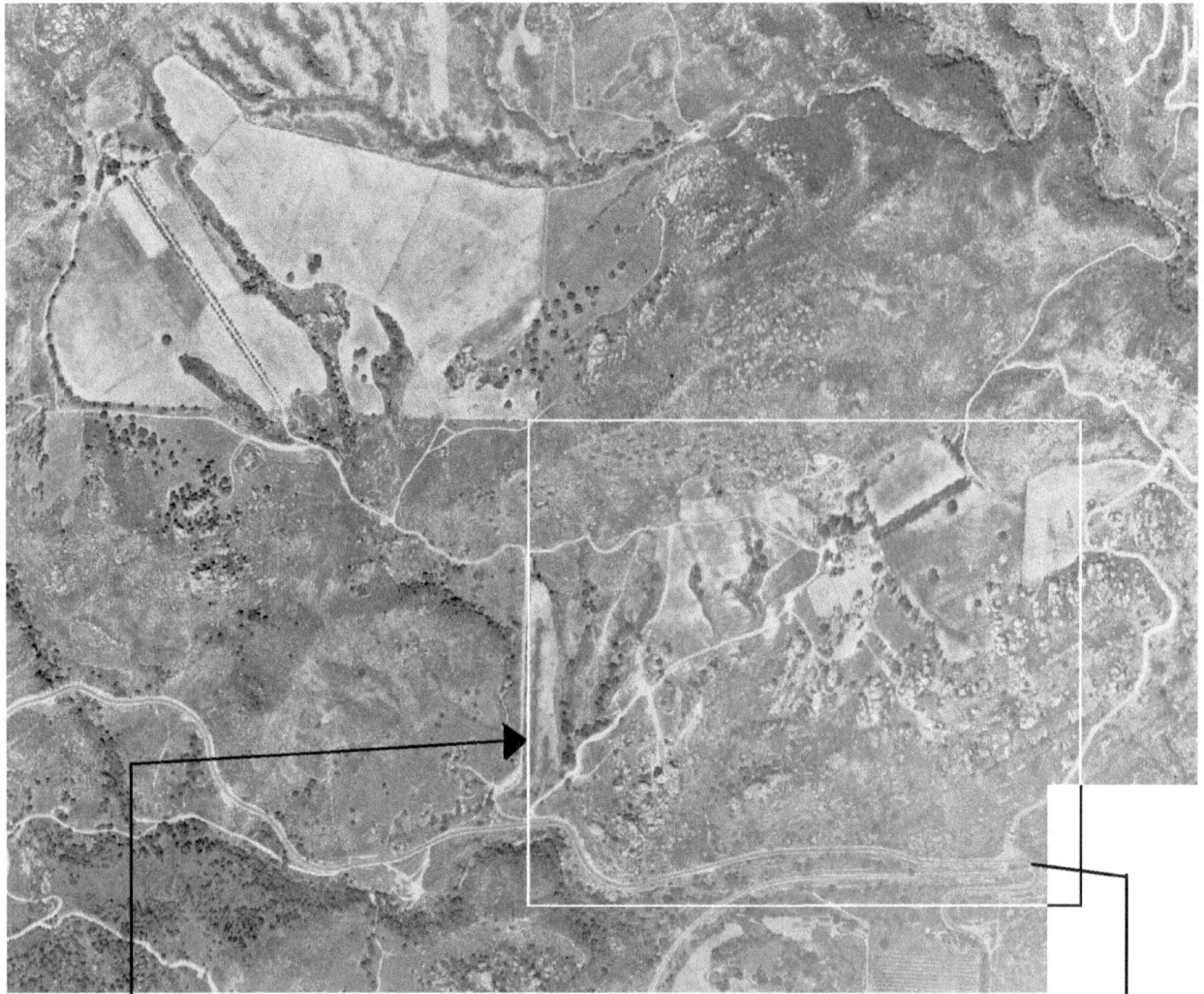

The Original Iverson Ranch Homestead Property
(as seen in a 1927 aerial photograph)

Iverson Movie Ranch 160 acre homestead
Santa Susana Pass Road

REAL LAND OF MAKE BELIEVE

Sitting on a rocky plateau in the Santa Susana Mountains overlooking the town of Chatsworth in the northwestern section of the San Fernando Valley, was a real ranch of make believe, the Iverson Movie Ranch.

Featured prominently at the original ranch site was and still is an area known as the Garden of the Gods (protected as parkland), possibly named by an unnamed silent film director, or possibly by one of the many visitors to the ranch during its lifetime. This ranch has featured a wide variety of make believe by actors and actresses of motion pictures, television shows, commercials, and photo shoots.

One day you could encounter World War II Japanese troops attacking the Seabees of John Wayne; or Errol Flynn's George Armstrong Custer and his cavalry fighting Crazy Horse and his Indians; or Bengal Lancers of Gary Cooper marching up the pass, or parading on the open ground of the Shirley Temple Wee Willie Winkie set; or encounter loin clothed Tarzan of the Apes, Bomba the Jungle Boy, or Kaspa the Lion Man; meeting superheroes such as Superman, Batman, and Captain Marvel; or comedians like Buster Keaton, The Three Stooges, Abbott & Costello, and Laurel & Hardy; or seeing Noah's Ark on top of the rocks; or facing Richard the Lion Hearted or Marco Polo; or shooting it out with The Lone Ranger and countless other western heroes and villains. The Iverson Movie Ranch filled the location wishes of a multitude of directors in thousands of films—the MOST photographed location ranch in film history.

The topography of the ranch could simulate any state, any condition, and any land, near or far. This was the Iverson Movie Ranch, owned and operated by the Iverson family.

Beginning with a 160 acre homestead, it gradually grew to two homesteads of 160 acres each and portions of another homestead. Ultimately, around 500 acres comprised this ranch.

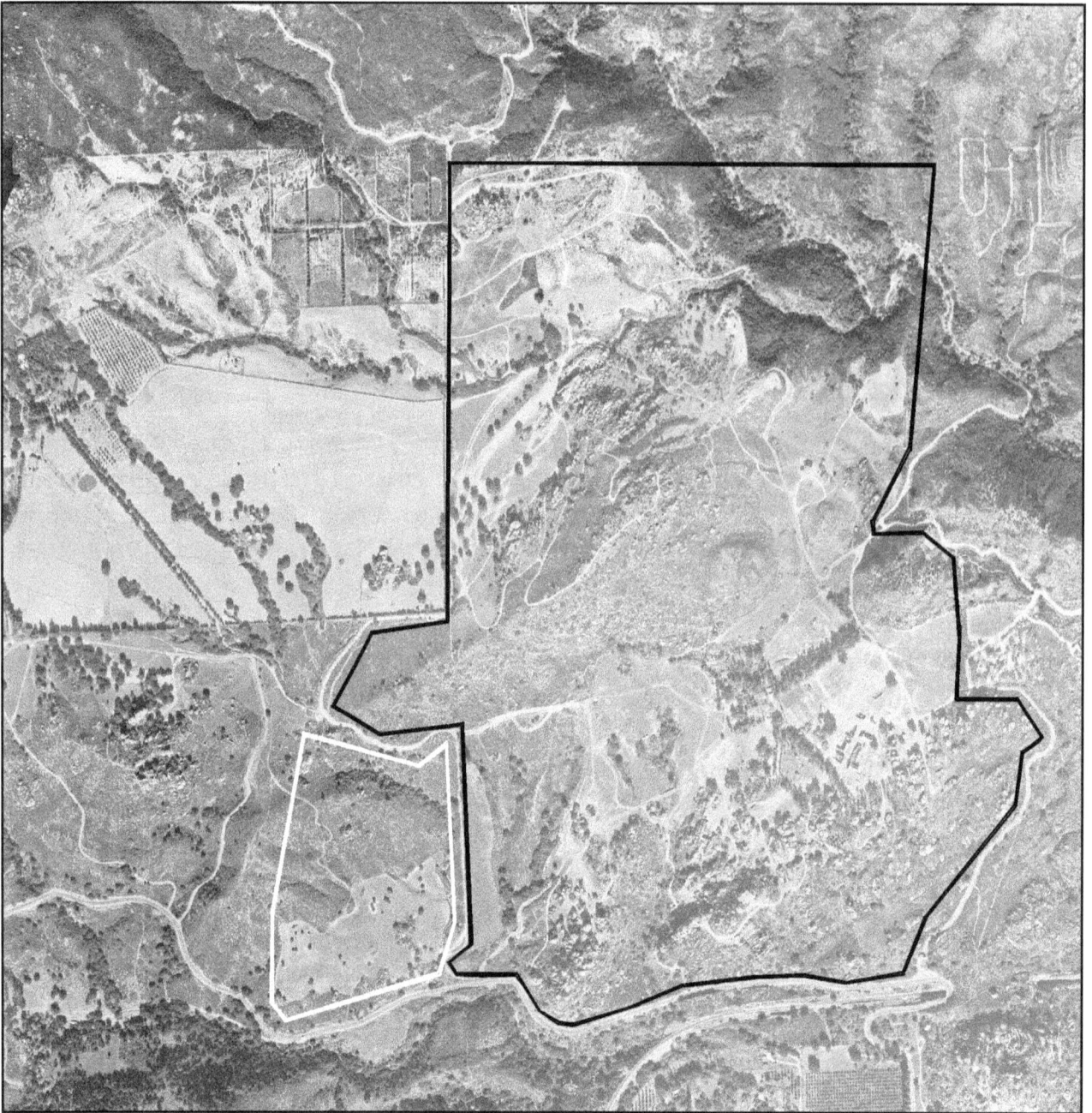

The Complete Iverson Movie Ranch Outlined in Black
White Outline may also have been part of the ranch
(1944 aerial photograph)

A look at how the ranch was transformed after development
(2018 Aerial Photograph)

Above: Household Examination Book (1881 to 1885) was the last entry for Augusta Mathilda Wagman who emigrated to America

Below: 1882 Ellis Island Immigration Record

THE BEGINNINGS

THE Steamship Furnessia arrived at Ellis Island in New York Harbor on May 16, 1882. Disembarking was a 25 year old single Swedish woman by the name of Augusta Mathilda Wågman. She was traveling alone. Augusta was born on December 26, 1856, at Fornås, Östergötland, Sweden. Her parentage is unknown at this time as no birth or baptism record has been located. Her birth date and place was recorded in the series of books kept by the church entitled "Household Examination Books". She is first found in the book for 1876 to 1880, and lastly in the book for 1881 to 1885. The books show that she moved from Fornås to

Steamship Furnessia

Lönsås in 1877. In 1881 she was living in Norrköpings. Sometime in late 1881 or early 1882, she traveled from Sweden to Glasgow, Scotland, where she boarded the SS Furnessia and headed to America to join her sister Caroline who had already emigrated and married (on July 16, 1876, in Coffey County, Kansas, to James Richard Williams). The Williams family is said to have arrived in Chatsworth, California, in 1881, and squatted on a piece of property in the Santa Susana hills (their property would be located adjacent on the south side of the Ann Wilden Johnson property, later to become the Brandeis Ranch, and on the west side of the land which would become the seminal Iverson Ranch). Squatting on federal land was permitted under the 1841 The Preemption Act which allowed squatters to purchase up to 160 acres at a very low price before the land was to be offered for sale to the general public. The Williams family were granted a homestead on the property in 1897.

When Augusta arrived in California, she headed to Chatsworth to be with her sister Caroline (also known as Carrie). Augusta was convinced to stay near them on the property directly to the east of theirs. Apparently, James Williams and Neils

Johnson (the squatter on the land to the north of the Williams) built a leanto for Augusta to live in.

Our story now heads back to Europe and Norway where Carl (Charles) Johan Iverson, the son of Iver Nielson and Kari Johannesdr, was born on March 17, 1860, in or near Horbabo, Horbaland, Norway. Apparently, Carl ran away from home at a young age and entered into the merchant seaman trade, sailing around the globe. While in this line of work, he heard stories about America and decided that he wished to move there. When given the opportunity to gain employment on a ship which would head to America, he quickly took it. After a long voyage, he landed at the port at San Pedro, California. Along with a shipmate, Johnny Peterson, they rented a room in Los Angeles and looked around for work. Carl finally found a job building a dam in Devil's Canyon on the Charlton Ranch in the hills above Chatsworth. He stated that it was hard work which lasted 6 days a week. On the seventh, he spent hunting and exploring the area. On one Sunday morning, he explored farther than before. Being tired and thirsty, he stumbled upon a leanto abode and knocked on the door. Augusta answered and that was the start of their friendship and eventual love story.

The marriage certificate of Charles Iverson and Augusta Wagman

On October 20, 1888, in Los Angeles County, California, they married. From that union, they had five children, all born at Chatsworth:

(1) Carl Isaac (a twin), born September 3, 1889; died December 10, 1960, Los Angeles, California; married Iva May White on December 28, 1915, at Long Beach, California.

(2) Anna Matilda (a twin), born September 3, 1889; died January 12, 1951, Chatsworth, California; married Leander A. Foss.

(3) Aaron Ephraim, born Jun 13, 1892; died May 9, 1973, Los Angeles, California; married Bessie Rogers Jacobs, August 30, 1933, Los Angeles, California.

(4) Joseph Adolph (a twin), born June 4, 1896; died November 7, 1986, Chatsworth, California; married (1) Cecile Louise Coffey, June 24, 1926, Los Angeles, California; after her death, married (2) Iva Mae Boyd.

(5) Sena Clara Marie (a twin), born June 4, 1896; died May 11, 1981, Ventura, California; married Frank Baker.

On November 25, 1892, Charles J. Iverson became a naturalized citizen.

In 1897, Charles J. Iverson was granted a homestead patent for the 160 acres of land which his wife, Augusta, had first squatted on. This land included property on the south side of the current Santa Susana Pass Road. When the Southern Pacific Railroad built its line from Chatsworth, through the Santa Susana Mountains to Simi Valley, they purchased from Charles J. Iverson for $60, a portion of his ranch on which the current railroad line runs from the tunnel under Topanga Canyon Blvd. westward to where it turns south (as reported on November 19, 1902, in *The Los Angeles Times* newspaper).

Marriage Photo of Charles and Augusta Iverson

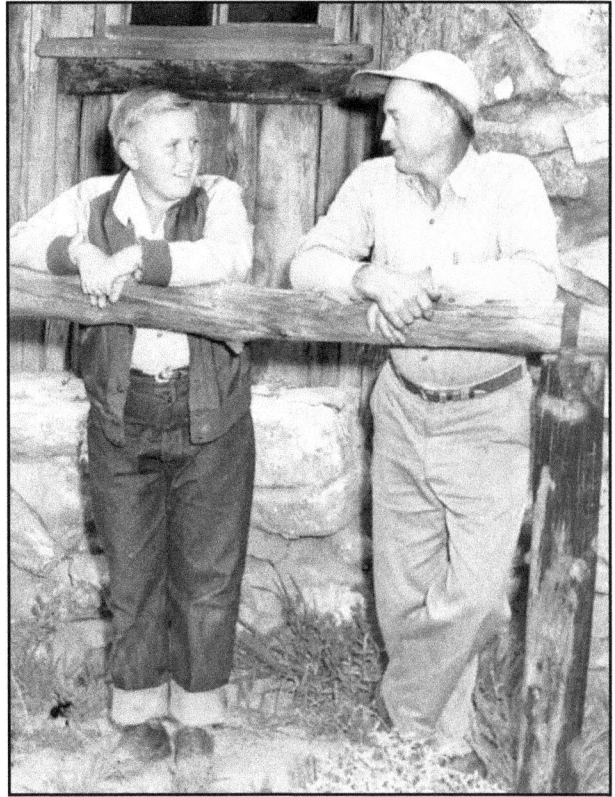

Above Left: Charles and Augusta in the 1940s
Above Right: Aaron and his son, Edwin
Below: Joseph and his second wife, Ida

GARDEN OF THE GODS

According to a story in a highly error-ridden book on the history of the movie ranch and from a newspaper account in the *Los Angeles Times* on November 28, 1926, the area of the ranch which became known as the Garden of the Gods, was so named because of its striking beauty and "just like the mountains in Colorado". Now, it was either because of a person from a film company early-on, or from conversations with visitors to the ranch, that the name was given to that area of the ranch. It is now one of the major features of the Garden of the Gods Park.

In 1895, a dirt road was built through Santa Susana Pass, just north of the old stagecoach road (Devil's Slide). It was called the New Santa Susanna Pass Road, but was later referred to as the Chatsworth Grade Road. It was this dirt road that the Iversons used to reach their ranch. Its original location was to the south of the current road through the pass. In 1917, the current road was built to the north of the old road, and was asphalt paved.

The main entrance road to the ranch passed just to the north of the rock formations in the Garden of the Gods, passed the Gorge rocks, and on to the ranch house (later houses as both Aaron and Joseph took up residences at the ranch, near each other, while the "old folks", Charles/Karl and Augusta lived on an overlook to the San Fernando Valley) where permission had to be obtained in order to either visit the ranch or to film on the ranch.

From the remembrances of Joseph Iverson, one day, early on, he found a portion of the wire fence around the ranch had been cut, so gathering up his rifle, he sat at that hole in the fence and awaited the return of whomever had cut it to gain free access to the ranch. Around about nightfall, a small group of people arrived to exit the ranch, the director in the lead. Joe told them that because they had entered the ranch illegally, the cost to film on it was increased with a penalty attached. The director stated that he didn't have the money to pay at that time, but would return the following day to pay up. Joe knew that wouldn't happen, so he told the director to leave all of the film equipment behind and when the director returned with the money, he could have the equipment. With his rifle in hand, the director knew he had to pay up, so he took up a collection from all of the film personnel and paid off Joe. That, apparently, was the last time a film company did not receive permission at the ranch house before beginning filming.

The following 8 pages show scenes from films shot at the Garden of the Gods.

Facing Page Top: An unidentified silent film
Facing Page Bottom: **Rimfire** (1949)

Above: A Charles Starrett publicity photo
Below: **Tarzan's Peril** (1951)

Man—Woman—Marriage

Starring

Dorothy Phillips

15

Above: **Noah's Ark** (1928)
The Ark is a matte painting.
Below: **Silver Treasure** (1926)

Richard the Lion Hearted (1923)
Top photo shows the set construction,
while the bottom photo shows what appeared
in the film

Above: **The Young Rajah** (1922)
Below: Have Gun Will Travel—The Long Night

Above: **Tarzan's Savage Fury** (1952)

Below: **Shut My Big Mouth** (1942)

A fake bridge was built at the Garden of the Gods for **Tell It to the Marines** (1926).

THE SILENT YEARS

How much filming took place at the ranch during the silent years (1912/14 to 1929) is mostly a question mark because, according to research recently done, seventy percent of all silent films are gone forever. Only thirty percent may still be available, whether in readily available format (dvds, film, etc.) or only in archives around the world. Of those, the earlier the film, the more difficult to determine if it was filmed at the ranch or at some other location in the vicinity (Chatsworth Park hills, which would now be the Chatsworth hills) because during the early years of filming at the ranch, the Iversons did little to make the use of the property easier or more photogenic for the production companies. But when they did, the transformation of the property was such that the early films are sometimes difficult to recognize the terrain.

What was the first film shot at the ranch? According to the recollection of Joe Iverson, as told to David Rothel, it is still unknown as the earliest film that Joe remembers was **The Squaw Man** (1914). [NOTE: There is a short sequence in the film which may have been shot at the ranch, but it is difficult to determine exactly where it was shot.] The problem of determining the name of the first film is two-fold:

(1) As a general rule, only the rocky section of the Lower Iverson was used for filming and those areas had not been turned into easy filming locations yet.

(2) Only 30% of silent films still survive and many of those are not available to the general public on dvd—they are still kept in a variety of archives around the world.

Added to reason 1 above, the Chatsworth Park (the original name for Chatsworth) area had many fine rock formations not unlike those found on the Iverson Ranch, and they were in easier reach from the flatlands of the San Fernando Valley. Because of this, early films such as **Man's Genesis** (1912) and **Brute Force** (1914) could have been filmed at Iverson or somewhere else in Chatsworth.

Facing Page Top: A publicity still from **Revenge** (1928)
Facing Page Bottom: A publicity still from **The Silent Man** (1917)

Above: Behind the scenes look at filming **Three Ages** (1923) with Buster Keaton
Below: **Balloonatic** (1923)

Above: **Flying Elephants** (1928) with Laurel & Hardy
Below: **Judith of Bethulia** (1914)

"WEE WILLIE WINKIE"

SHIRLEY TEMPLE and VICTOR McLAGLEN share in the adventures of the Black Watch in "Wee Willie Winkie," in which they have been co-starred by 20th Century-Fox.

with England's greatest men, in the Poet's Corner of Westminster Abbey. There, under a plain stone, simply inscribed, "RUDYARD KIPLING, 1865-1936," lies the great writer who summed up the experiences and end of every man in his "Recessional";

"The tumult and the shouting dies;
The captains and the Kings depart . . ."

In addition to drawing on his own experiences for the story of "Wee Willie Winkie," Kipling ornamented the tale—as he did with all his stories—with the priceless wisdom which he gleaned from "all sorts of people, from priests in Chubara, from Ala Yar the carver, Jiwun Singh the carpenter, women spinning outside their cottages in the twilight, officers and gentlemen now dead and buried."

But he was more than a master of the technique of story telling, he was also a great innovator. In some of the methods of story-telling he perfected the anticipated devices which were to prove effective in film-making. The death of his son in the war and the feeling that he was no longer understood, that new generations were less easily moved by the saga of imperialism, however, sent him into a strange, self-imposed seclusion. Film technicians are inclined to think that otherwise he might not have refused the many tempting calls which came to him from the film industry. Motion pictures have appealed strongly to many another writer who came to maturity in his craft before the influence of films as a medium of expression could be felt. Among these are such prominent names as H. G. Wells, now an enthusiast for films as a means of conveying ideas he entrusted, formerly, only to the printed page; Hugh Walpole, W. J. Locke and the late John Galsworthy,

At an isolated spot in the rocky Santa Susanna Mountains, where nature provided a geographic replica of India's famous Khyber Pass, only 40 miles from Hollywood, his Indian frontier of 1898 was reproduced in faithful detail in a series of 34 permanent outdoor sets which sprawled over an area one-mile square in the rock-strewn mountains.

The sets ranged from crude stone look-outs of fierce Pathan warriors to

RUDYARD KIPLING chronicled the growth of the greatest of modern empires. In verse and prose he charted the march of British destiny across five continents and on the seven seas. And he it was, who better than any other writer—living or dead—described the growth of British dominion in the most colourful field of British imperial adventure—India.

Kipling knew India as few natives do. He knew its Maharajahs, its fakirs, its priests, and peasants—its kindly villagers, the furtive animal inhabitants of its jungles, and the fierce Pathan warriors who still inhabit the difficult mountain passes of its mighty Himalayas.

But of all the stories Kipling wrote concerning this fascinating land of his birth, none is more representative of his genius and of India than the story of "Wee Willie Winkie."

Rudyard Kipling's books occupy a prominent place in household libraries throughout the English-speaking world; in America alone, during the past 40 years, more than three and

a half million volumes of his works have been sold.

When men and women look back on the exciting events of their childhood, they remember the happy hours spent in the company of "Mowgli," the wolf-boy of the "Jungle Books," with "Kim, the little friend of all the world," and with "Wee Willie Winkie," the child of British India, who inflamed an entire regiment of Highlanders with a demonstration of unbelievable courage.

Historians say that Kipling loved the story of "Wee Willie Winkie" above all his other great works, because it depicted some of his own childhood. It is this story that 20th Century-Fox has made into the cinema production which stars Shirley Temple as "Wee Willie Winkie." With scrupulous care, producers, film technicians, writers, and research men laboured for over a year under the direction of Darryl F. Zanuck, Vice-President in charge of production, in order that the film story might reproduce in minutest detail the stirring scenes which Kipling described.

Kipling was born in India in 1865, the son of the director of the Bombay Art School. Educated in England, he returned to Lahore, India, at the age of 17, to work on the editorial

staff of "The Civil and Military Gazette."

At 21 he had collected his "Departmental Ditties," and by 1887 he was beginning to publish his "Tales of India," the first volume of which was "Plain Tales." Subsequently he wrote and published "The Jungle Books," the "Just So Stories," "Kim," "Stalky & Co.," as well as dozens of other volumes, which have secured

Jean Holt writes of the genius of Kipling and the film of his favourite story

him an undying and unique reputation as a story-teller.

In 1907 Kipling received the highest honour that the world can bestow upon a writer—the Nobel Prize for Literature.

Few of those who have read and loved the works of Kipling realise that his wife was an American. On a visit to America, Kipling met and married a Vermont girl—Caroline Starr Balestier.

The creator of "Wee Willie Winkie" died in 1936. He was the third man in the Twentieth Century to be buried

the headquarters of an entire regiment of Scottish Highlanders, but before the Director. John Ford, could bring in Shirley Temple and Victor McLaglan and the rest of the important cast of the picture, construction crews had to create what was literally a subsidiary studio at the site. First there were roads to be built, and then a two-acre parade ground to level. Then came the erection of shelter for a permanent staff—and the construction of 15 behind-the-scenes buildings: a make-up department capable of accommodating 15 players at once, a field hospital for the minor injuries

1937

As each year of the 1930s decade came and went, more movies were filmed each subsequent year than the year before. By the time 1937 arrived, 1936 had been the most filmed year at the ranch. Then Shirley Temple and company arrived and life at the ranch greatly changed.

It was in late January of 1937 that 20th Century-Fox brought their production team to the ranch. They built a series of faithful replicas of 1898 Indian frontier buildings over a one-mile square area, with sets ranging from crude stone lookouts of fierce Pathan warriors to the headquarters of an entire regiment of Scottish Highlanders. But before the actors arrived, construction crews also had to create a mini-studio. First, there were roads to build, and then a two-acre parade ground to level. Then the erection of shelter for a permanent staff and the construction of 15 behind-the-scenes buildings: a make-up department capable of accommodating 15 players at once, a field hospital for the minor injuries, a light generating plant, stables for 150 horses, shelter for goats and camels, a gigantic mess hall, dressing rooms, a property room, and other vital structures (as reported in the December 1, 1937, issue of *The Queenslander*). "Important, too, was the regiment of 1000 Scottish Highlanders, the famed "Black Watch," which had to be wardrobed and trained to the perfection of crack troops."

A half a mile from the cluster of buildings which comprised the army cantonment, a native mountain village and fort were built—the stronghold of Khoda Khan. And a third cluster of buildings were erected on a peak, and "up a narrow road toiled tractors with heavy camera and lighting equipment to photograph the important scenes of Shirley Temple and C. Aubrey Smith at the durbar of Khoda Khan."

Shirley Temple's trailer, where she lived during 2 months of filming at the ranch for her scenes, was located near Joe Iverson's home. It is said that the Temple family loved the location so much, they wished to purchase the land.

And it was sometime during this year in which they expanded their property by purchasing the Frank Raposo homestead (160 acres) directly north of their homestead.

A 1927 aerial photograph showing the Lower Iverson (lower right quarter of image) and the Brandeis Ranch (upper left quarter)

Original entrance road to Fern Ann Springs through the Frank Raposo Homestead Property which crossed over Fern Ann Creek at the bridge (see Movie Sets Section)

Fern Ann Springs

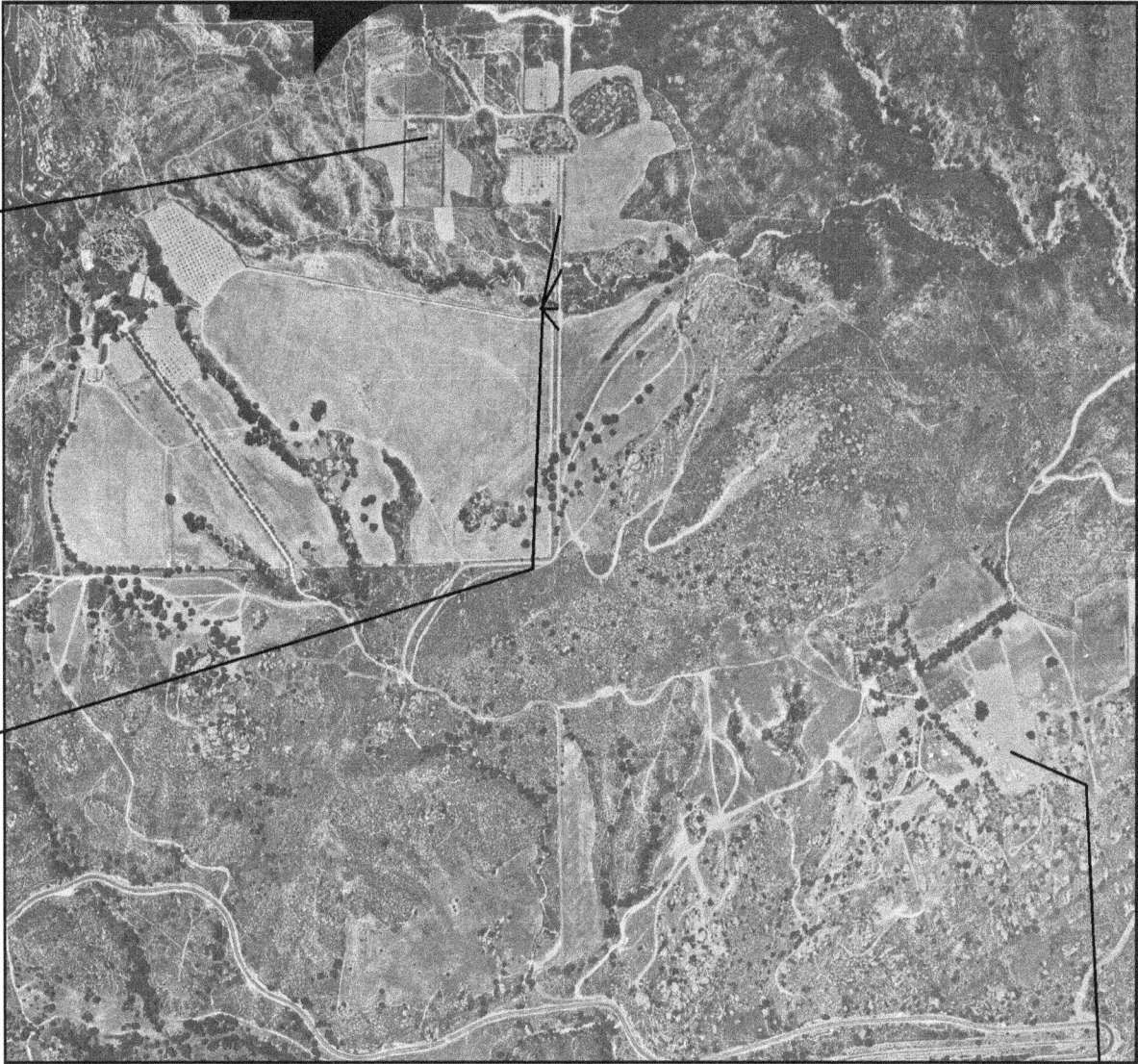

A 1937 aerial photograph showing the Lower Iverson (lower right quarter of image) with the Wee Willie Winkie sets in place in the Sheep Flats area and the Brandeis Ranch (upper left quarter)

The original entrance road to Fern Ann Springs has been extended straight north. Insert roads have been added to the new Upper Iverson property.

Fern Ann Springs

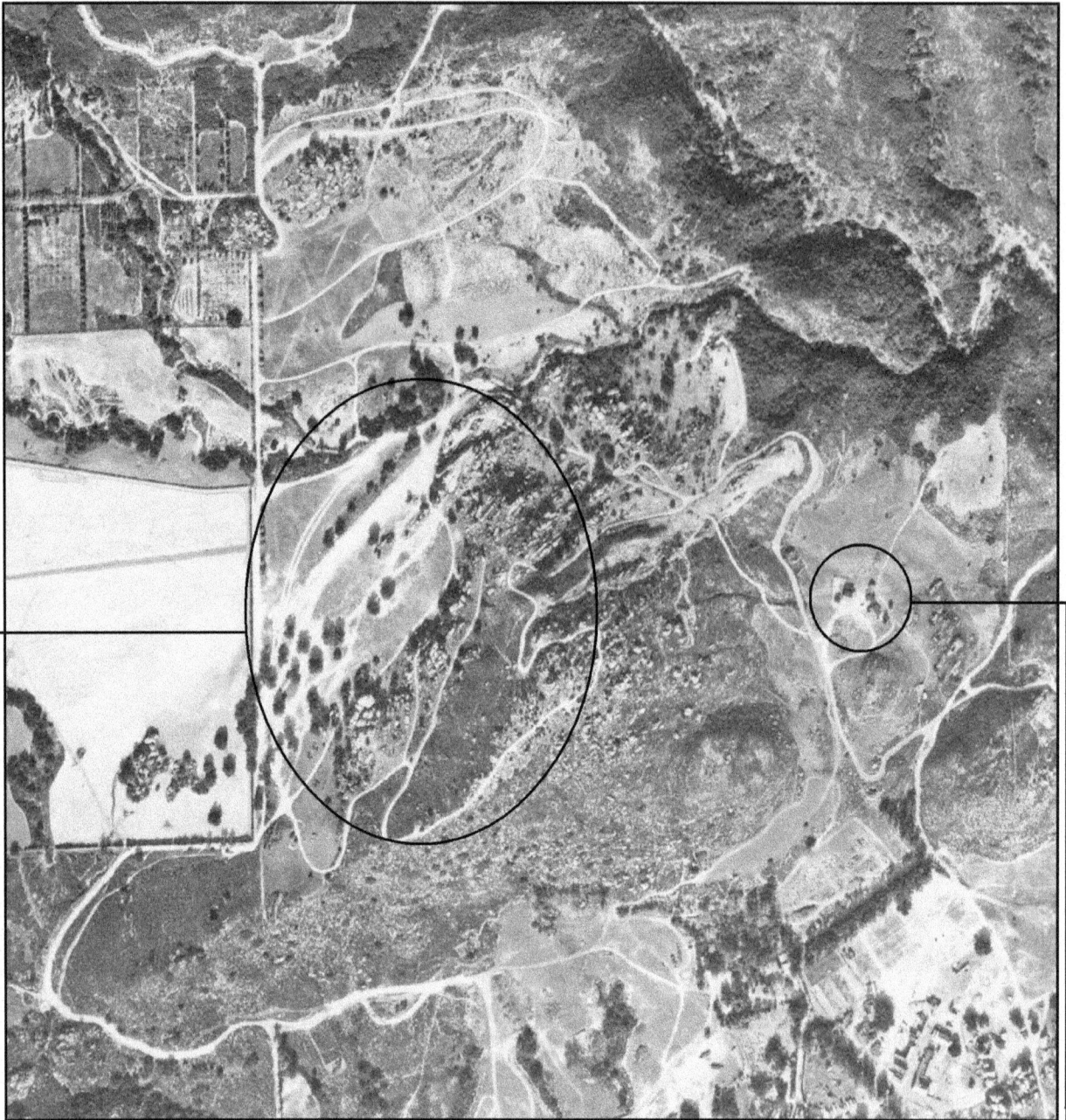

A 1944 Aerial Photograph showing the Upper Iverson
and portions of the Lower Iverson and the Brandeis Ranch

More Insert Roads in place

Middle Iverson Ranch Set

THE WEE WILLIE WINKIE SET TRANSITION

The **Wee Willie Winkie** Indian Army Fort set was built in early 1937. Over the coming years, it was added to and redressed, and had portions removed. In 1944, the western town set for **Along Came Jones** removed major portions of the set. The accompanying aerial photographs show the progression of the set from 1937 until it was completely gone in 1965 (enclosed in **black** lines). At the same time, you can also see the progression of the western street set from 1944 to 1958 (enclosed in gray lines).

1937

1944

1938

1945

1946 1956

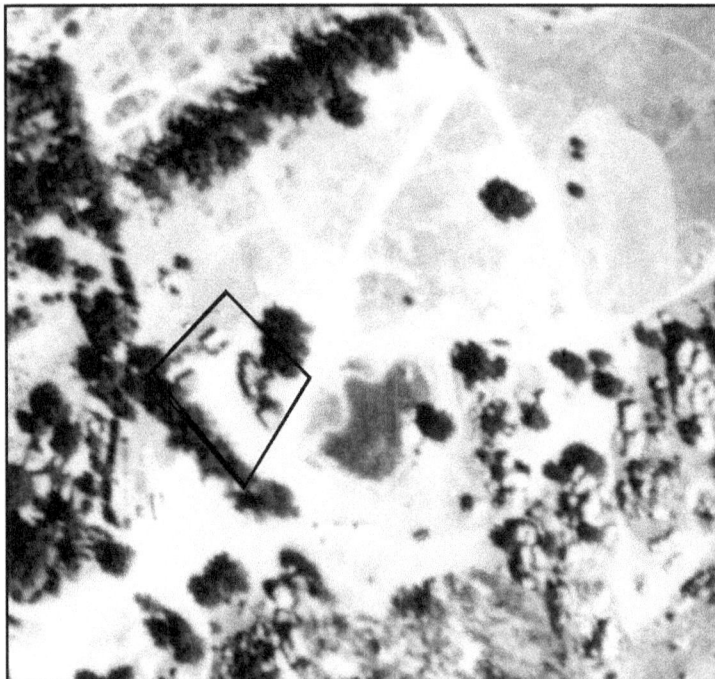
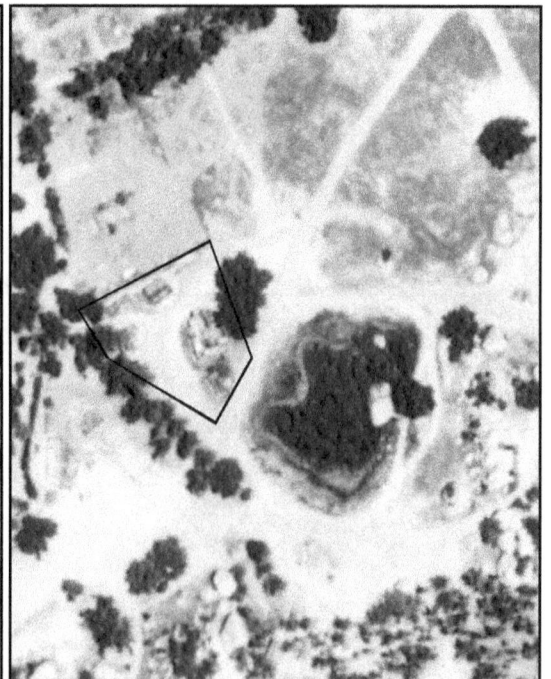

1958 1960

By 1965, the Sheep Flats area where the **Wee Willie Winkie** and the **Along Came Jones** sets had been located were completely removed, the property sold off, and a trailer park took over the area.

1943-1944

Even with the advent of World War II, film productions at the ranch continued to increase, mostly westerns. During the months of September to December 1943, Republic Pictures invaded the ranch to film **The Fighting Seabees** (1944), starring John Wayne. Major areas of the ranch were used for filming the picture including the Garden of the Gods, Nyoka Cliff, Lower Iverson Gorge, and the insert road area of the Upper Iverson which was transformed into a landing strip for airplanes.

Then, in 1944, Gary Cooper brought his production company to the ranch and built a western town in the Sheep Flats section—the same section where the **Wee Willie Winkie** Indian fort had been built. The western set was built on an angle in a northeast/southwest alignment, and several structures of the **Wee Willie Winkie** set had to be removed. The set was completed by November 21 as seen in 1944 aerial photographs (see page 31) and the production had already begun filming on the movie in early November. The film was released in 1945.

Most of this new set was merely false fronts, while one or two were actual structures in which interior filming could be performed.

Over the next thirteen years, the set was expanded and reconfigured (single story buildings becoming two stories, different sets removed and added, and for a few years, a church/school house appeared at the southern end of town. (For more information about the western street set, see the Movie Sets section of this book.]

The Upper Iverson, by 1944, already had many of its insert roads ready for filming, and several sets had been built, including the Stone Cabin. A real ranch house was built in an area due north of the Sheep Flats area, in an area I refer to as the Middle Iverson. The house was used by ranch workers to live in.

In the following decade, further sets were erected on the Upper Iverson, including the Fury Set, the Midway House, the Lone Ranger/Miner's Cabin, and the Upper Iverson Western Town (see the Movie Sets section for information on these sets).

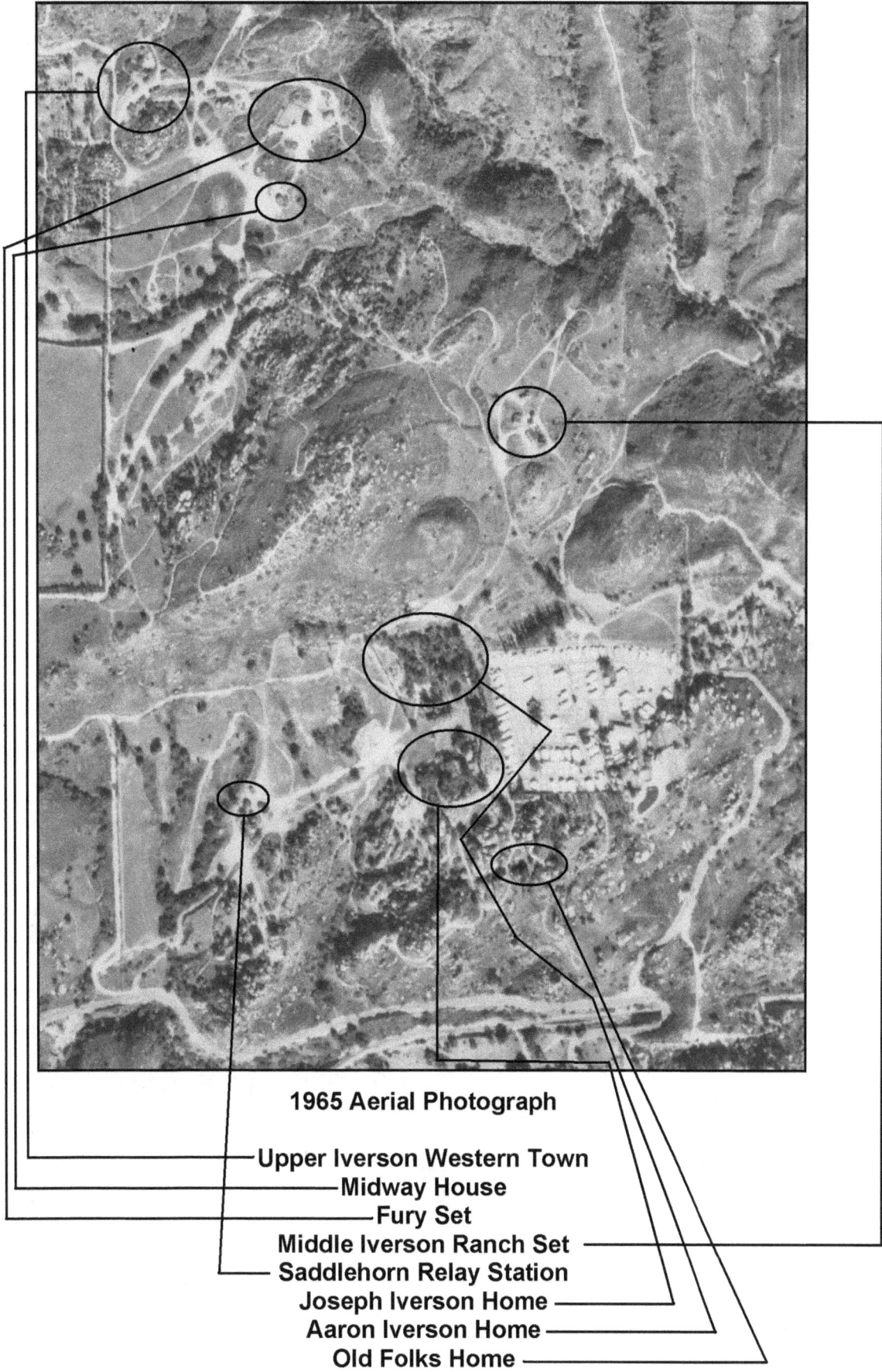

1965 Aerial Photograph

Upper Iverson Western Town
Midway House
Fury Set
Middle Iverson Ranch Set
Saddlehorn Relay Station
Joseph Iverson Home
Aaron Iverson Home
Old Folks Home

Mrs. Agusta Matilda Iverson, 65 Years in Chatsworth, Laid to Rest Yesterday

Agusta Matilda Iverson, 91, who took up the homestead around which was developed the famed Iverson ranch in Chatsworth, was buried yesterday in Oakwood Cemetery beside her husband, Carl J. Iverson, who died last year.

Mrs. Iverson passed away Sunday at her ranch home, and the funeral service was conducted at 10:30 a.m. in Oakwood Chapel under direction of Praiswater Funeral Home.

Her maiden name was Agusta Wogman, and she was born on Dec. 26 nearly 92 years ago, in Noorkoping, Sweden.

As a girl in her teens she came to the United States, stopping first with relatives in Nebraska and later coming to relatives in California.

About 65 years ago she married Carl Iverson and settled on the 160-acre homestead she had obtained from the government.

Three sons survive. They are Carl of Chatsworth, Joseph and Aaron of the ranch, the two latter having been partners with their mother and father in building up the mountain home which now consists of approximately 640 acres of picturesque terrain on which motion picture companies frequently shoot western scenes.

Surviving also are two daughters, Mrs. Anna Foss of Chatsworth and Mrs. Sena Baker of Canoga Park; six grandchildren and five great grandchildren.

Early Valley Settler Dies

CHATSWORTH, Oct. 5—Mrs. Carl Iverson, 91-year-old early day valley settler, died today at her famed ranch home here.

Mrs. Iverson came to this area 72 years ago from Sweden. Born Augusta Mathilda Wogman, she became the wife of Carl Iverson, and they homesteaded 160 acres.

Their holdings accumulated to 3000 acres and today the original ranch still remains, managed by their two sons, Aaron and Joseph. The ranch has become noted as a motion picture location. Iverson died a year ago.

In addition to the two sons, Mrs. Iverson leaves another son, Carl of Chatsworth; two daughters, Mrs. Anna Foss of Chatsworth and Mrs. Sena Baker of Canoga Park; and an older sister, Mrs. Terry Williams, 96, of Chatsworth.

Funeral services will be conducted at 10:30 a.m. tomorrow at Oakwood Cemetery Chapel here.

CHARLES JOHN IVERSON, 87 died Thursday on his ranch in Chatsworth. The funeral service was held this morning in the Oakwood Cemetery chapel under direction of the Praiswater Funeral Home. He homesteaded the Chatsworth ranch in 1885 and had lived there since that time. Surviving him are his wife, his sons Carl, Aaron and Joseph, and a daughter Mrs. Anna Foss all of Chatsworth and a daughter Mrs. Sena Baker of Canoga Park. Also surviving are six grandchildren and four great grandchildren.

THE END OF THE BEGINNING

The first part of the history of the ranch was fast coming to an end. On September 4, 1947, Charles (Karl) Johan Iverson died. A little over a year later, his wife, Augusta Matilda Wagman Iverson died—October 3, 1948. Both were buried at the Oakwood Memorial Park at Chatsworth, California.

Despite the death of their parents, the ranch had, for many years, been under the control of the two brothers who also resided on the property in an area adjacent to the west of the Sheep Flats section.

Rental fees for the ranch varied depending on the studio, the number of people involved in the shoot, sets used, animals used, etc. In a 1937 newspaper article, it stated that "Mr. Iverson has a sound system of charging his clients. They pay as much as they can afford. Western companies producing "quickies" give only $150 per day per camera to photograph in and about the ranch. But a company like Samuel Goldwyn's, for instance, finds itself spending around $24,000 a day—an average of 1,000 people costing $5 per person for food, $1.50 transportation, $2.50 costume, and $15 for technicians and extras. This sum does not include the cost of erecting the sets, production expenditures, electricity, water, the salaries of stars. Iverson's price system is so tangled with whimsical eccentricities, an army of bookkeepers is required to add and check up. "The Adventures of Marco Polo" company, with Gary Cooper starred, was charged 50 cents per day for each of the 400 extras before the latter were allowed on the property. One hundred fifty horses set Mr. Goldwyn back 25 cents per head. Light vehicles were admitted for $1 each; trucks cost $2 each, and $100 was demanded for each camera and generaator." In a 1941 newspaper article, it is mentioned that "Iverson's $50 rate applies when the company is actually working. He [Aaron] gets $25 a day when sets are being built or torn down, and $15 a day for "dead storage" or days on which the sets are idle while the company works at the studio."

Above: **California** (1946)
Below: **The Marauders** (1947)

MOVIE SETS

Location ranches which belonged to studios, generally had standing sets which were, more or less, permanent. Major independent location ranches sometimes built standing sets which were semi-permanent, or allowed production companies to build on their land and then kept those sets standing after filming had been completed. But those sets wouldn't be semi-permanent or permanent, but would only last as long as other production companies used them and enhanced them. The Corrigan Movie Ranch (Corriganville) and the Ingram Movie Ranch had permanent sets (their western towns) which the owners of those ranches built. Like the Iverson Movie Ranch, Corrigan also allowed production companies to build sets on his property and leave them behind for others to use. Fort Apache and the Corsican Village were two such examples.

The Iverson family built a few minor sets, but most all of the major sets were built by production companies and the Iversons allowed the sets to remain standing afterwards. Some stood for a short time, others for several years. None of the sets on their ranch were permanent sets except for the Fury Sets and the Midway House. All others were either semi-permanent or not supposed to last too many years without upkeep (and upkeep on sets was performed by production companies wishing to use the sets).

When a production company built a set at the ranch and it remained standing after they finished shooting, the Iversons had a policy of not allowing any other production company to use that set for one year's time. For instance, the adobe fort which was built for **Wee Willie Winkie** was used from January to March 1937. The next company to use it was Republic Pictures in May 1938, just over a year later, for **Army Girl**. RKO next used the set in July/September 1938 for **Renegade Ranger**. Then Republic returned again in September/October 1938 for **Storm Over Bengal**.

We will look at some of the sets which were built and remained standing after filming.

LOWER IVERSON — SADDLEHORN RELAY STATION

Originally named the Squaw Creek Relay Station for the 1940 film **Ghost Valley Raiders**, it first appeared quite close in proximity to the Batman Rock near the Garden of the Gods. Then, within a year's time, it had been relocated to its final location as seen in **Hands Across the Rockies** in 1941. The relay station outward appearance changed over the years as different production companies added to its looks. In the late 1950s, several buildings were added to the location in what we refer to as Saddlehorn Village. Apparently first used in **Escort West** in 1958. The relay station building was one of the few sets to survive the fires at the ranch and was torn down in the 1970s.

The original location of the relay station in 1940 on the main Iverson Entrance road, next to the Batman Rock. By the next year, the set had been relocated across the road and northwest a short ways (see top image on next page).

Bottom:
Hands Across the Rockies (1941)

Top: **Black Bart** (1948) — East Side of Relay Station
Bottom: **Texans Never Cry** (1951) — South Side

By the late 1950s, a small village was built near the relay station
(**Escort West** – 1959)

A portion of the village set
(*The Life and Legend of Wyatt Earp —*
The Fanatic — November 20, 1960)

The relay station was still standing after the 1970 wildfire.
The photo above was taken in the mid-1970s.

LOWER IVERSON — GORGE CABIN AND MINE

Located in the gorge between Nyoka Cliff and the Garden of the Gods, for a period from about 1936 into 1944, was a four-sided cabin (a shell, not a false front). Around 1940, a small addition was built on the left side (if you are facing the front of the cabin). A little later, another addition was built onto the left side addition. In 1944, the gorge cabin disappeared, but a similar looking cabin appeared on the Upper Iverson that same year. Just to the east of the cabin was the Gorge Arch (see the Rocks Section), and to the east of that was a fake mine entrance.

Above: The complete cabin (**Holt of the Secret Service** 1941)
Bottom: The fake cave entrance

After the Gorge Cabin disappeared in 1944, an Indian adobe village appeared in the same general vicinity. It remained in place until about 1954.

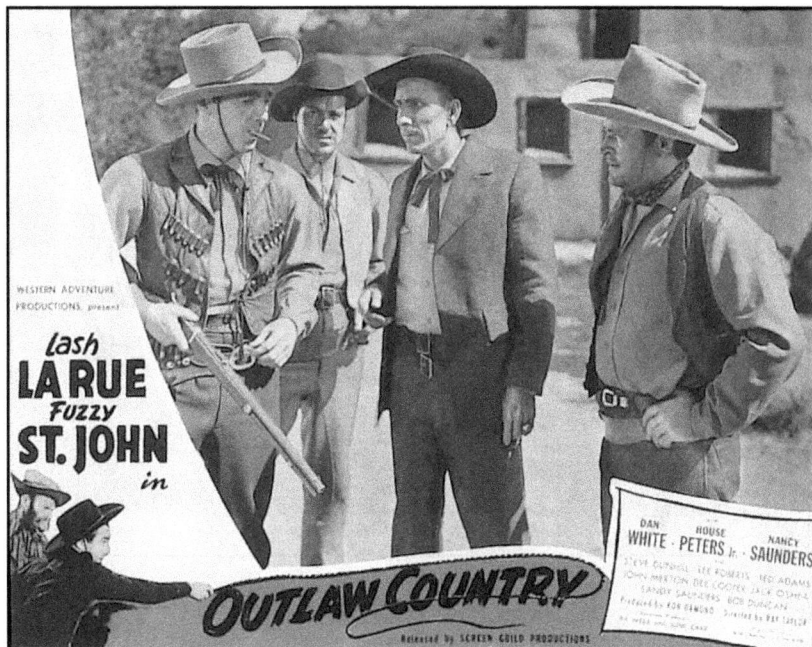

Top: Part of the set circa 1950
Bottom: **Outlaw Country** (1949)

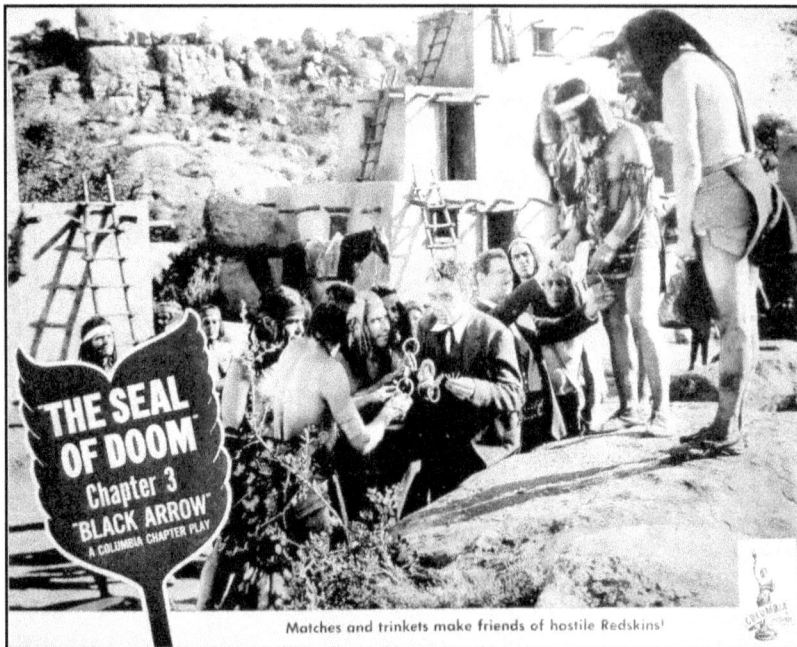

Matches and trinkets make friends of hostile Redskins!

Black Arrow (1944)

Two large sets were built in the Upper Gorge region: the Mogala set for **The Lives of a Bengal Lancer** (1934) and the Khoda Khan stronghold in **Wee Willie Winkie** (1937). Remnants of this latter set remained for a few years and appeared **The Phantom** (1941), among others.

The Mogala set
The Lives of a Bengal Lancer (1934)

The Mogala set with Joseph Iverson

Behind the Scenes
Shots of the **Wee Willie Winkie** set (1937)

Above: Filming of a scene in **Wee Willie Winkie** (1937)

Bottom: A view of the interior of the stronghold
(**Wee Willie Winkie** 1937)

Above: **Holt of the Secret Service** (1941)
Below: **Wild Stallion** (1952)

Built for 1942s **Perils of Nyoka** by Republic Pictures, it was a false front structure blocking a roadway in the cliffs near to Nyoka Cliff and Hole in the Wall— Hangover Rock was just behind the set. The set remained in place for a few years as it can be seen in the background of unrelated films.

Perils of Nyoka (1942)

Facing Page Top: **Perils of Nyoka** (1942)
Facing Page Bottom: **Daredevils of the West** (1943)—
Vultura's Palace can be seen directly above the saddle horn of the horse

Located in the hill to the west of the Gorge, there is a rock which overhangs the dirt road. Underneath that rock, there used to be a cabin built into the side of the hill. It is seen in **Batman and Robin** as well as **Cripple Creek** among other films and television shows. It was probably the last set to remain standing at the ranch. I saw it in 1993, but others have seen it as late as 1998.

Above: **Outlaws of Boulder Pass** (1942)

Left: **Buffalo Bill Rides Again** (1947)

Above: **Superman** (1948) landing via animation

Below: Near the end of its life—photo taken in 1993

LOWER IVERSON — GROVE CABIN AND MINE

Over near the Sheep Flats area of the Lower Iverson is a grove of eucalyptus trees. Quite close to those trees and out of sight of the western street, from about 1939 to 1958 was a cabin. For a few years, there was a fake mine entrance located nearby to the right of the cabin (looking at the cabin from the front). By 1956, a second cabin had been added to the right of the main cabin.

Above: The original cabin in 1939 with the original roof
Below: The updated roof

Above: The fake mine entrance (middle of photo)
Below: The second cabin added, hiding the fake mine

For a few years, from at least 1946 to at least 1958, there was a relay station in the grove area, located a little ways to the left of the Grove Cabin.

Above: **The Fighting Frontiersman** (1946)
Below: The Rifleman—Skull (the pond in the middle background was located in the middle of where the western town was situated

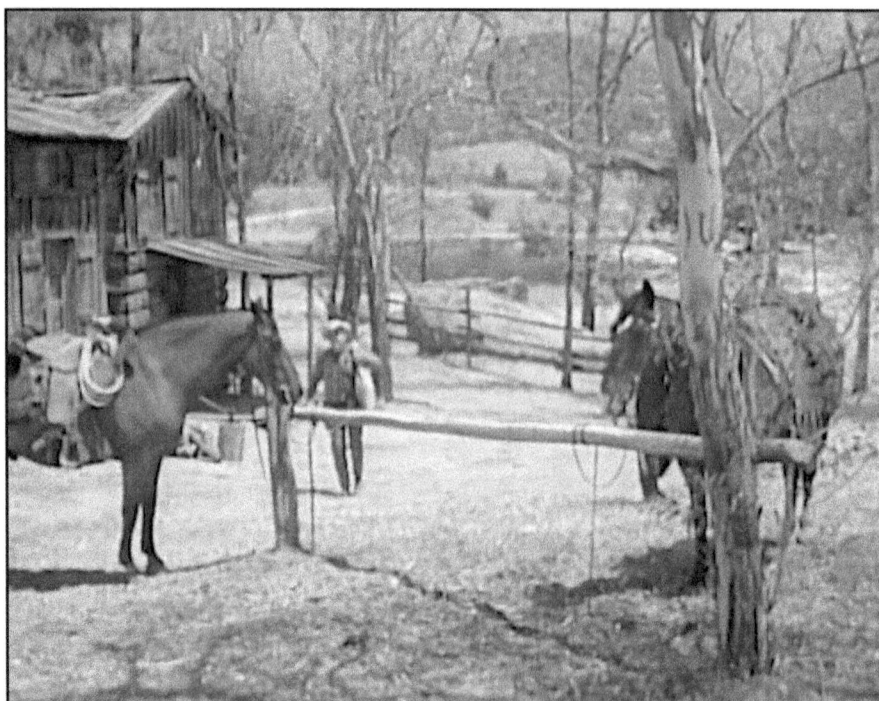

LOWER IVERSON — WEE WILLIE WINKIE BENGAL FORT

In 1937, 20th Century-Fox built a large compound for a Bengal Fort for **Wee Willie Winkie**. Additions to the set were in place by 1944, but were removed in late 1945 or early 1946. The main fort set remained in place until 1945 when it was replaced by the western street. The remaining sets remained until the Sheep Flats area was sold off for a trailer park. Those remaining sets, were used in many types of films, including an African jungle film (**The Hidden City** with Bomba), Arab desert film (**The Desert Hawk**), Mongolia (**State Department: File 649**), and many westerns.

The main fort set, located in the southeast section of Sheep Flats (seen here in **Army Girl** 1938) was removed when the western street set was erected in 1945 (this would be the south end of the town)

Above: The **Wee Willie Winkie** set
Below: Looking northwest in the Sheep Flats section,
the sets being to the left and behind the camera position

Above: Filming **Wee Willie Winkie** in early 1937
Below: Shirley Temple and Victor McLaglen

Two views of the same set, filmed a few months apart by Columbia Pictures—
top view is from 1944's **Desert Hawk** and the bottom view is from
1944's **Black Arrow**

The above sets were built for an unknown film, but were used in the Columbia serial **De-sert Hawk** in 1944. These sets were removed around 1945/46, after the western town had been erected and filming completed on **Along Came Jones**.

Above: Joe Iverson looking after the **Wee Willie Winkie** sets which were still standing in 1948
Below: The Wee Willie Winkie sets in 1952s Bomba film **Hidden City**

LOWER IVERSON — WESTERN STREET

Built by Gary Cooper's production company for the 1945 movie **Along Came Jones** (see photo below). To accommodate the set in the Sheep Flats area, the two main buildings of the **Wee Willie Winkie** set were removed. The western street was then built on a diagonal setting, northeast/southwest. The northern end of the street stopped at a few of the **Wee Willie Winkie** sets and later additions to that set. These latter sets were removed by 1947 when additional new buildings were incorporated into the western town set, probably at the same time as the addition of a church/school house on the south end of town for **The Millerson Case** (gone by 1951). Also for that film, the Rainbow Mine Co. was added to the south end of town on the west side. About 1949, the Casa Grande false front building was added at the north end of the town. When the rodeo arena was built to the north of the town in 1953, the Casa Grande building hid the arena from view except for careless camera positioning in which case some of the wooden arena fence walls can be seen. The town was gone by 1958 and replaced by a water pond feature (the area naturally filled with water when it rained).

Along Came Jones

Top: The western street in 1948 (looking southward)
Bottom: **Gold Raiders** (1951) (looking northward)

Top: Looking north in **The Daltons' Women** (1950)
Bottom: **Man From Sonora** (1951)

Both images this page:
Behind the scenes of *Annie Oakley*
Episode *Tuffy*
Filmed in 1956

Top: The corrals on the southeast side of the western street
Bottom: This film capture shows how close some of the **Wee Willie Winkie** sets were to the back side of the west side of the western street

UPPER IVERSON — MIDDLE IVERSON RANCH SET

This ranch set was in place around 1940 to 1942. It consisted of a real ranch house with fronts of the west side and east side, and a secondary entrance on the north side. I met one of the occupants of the house back in the 1990s. They worked at the ranch and lived in the ranch house. This house was gone by 1969.

The first barn was built around the same time as the ranch house, but it was rarely seen on film. It was gone by October 23, 1945, when an aerial photograph of the ranch was taken.

The bunkhouse was built about 1946 and lasted until the 1970 fire.

The cottage survived for most of the life of the ranch set. It can be seen to good advantage in 1945s **Rough Riders of Cheyenne**.

The second barn was built between 1956 and 1958. It can be seen in 1961s **Gun Street**.

The above screen capture from *Wanted Dead or Alive's* episode of *Dead End*, you see the second barn on the left, the barracks just to its right, and the southwest facing side of the ranch house.

Above: The first barn as seen in **Bells of Rosarita** (1945)

Below: The second barn as seen in **Gun Street** (1961)

Above: A view of the cottage sitting between the ranch house on the left (the southeast view) and the barracks (partially seen on the right of the cottage (*The Lone Ranger,—Courage of Tonto*)

Below: The barracks (*Have Gun Will Travel—Show of Force*)

Above: The rarely used third entrance to the ranch house (north side) (**Hostile Country** 1950)

Below: Looking northwest from the ranch house—the roadway leading down to the ranch from the hill (seen behind the riders, slanting downwards) was paved with asphalt, then covered with dirt for filming (**Colorado Ranger** 1950)

UPPER IVERSON — FURY SET

After five episodes shot at Idyllwild, the *Fury* television show moved its location work to the Iverson Ranch where a large barn had been built in 1955, located in the northern section of the Upper Iverson. The Midway House, which was built in 1956 and was used as the ranch house for *Fury*, is featured next. By 1958, a house was built near the barn, but was rarely seen in the *Fury* show, but was seen in other shows. This set burned in the 1970 fire.

The entrance to the *Fury* set with the *Fury* barn and corral (*Have Gun Will Travel—Young Gun*)

Above: The house at the *Fury* set (*Have Gun Will Travel—Juliet*)

Below: A closeup of the front of the house

Above: The *Fury* cabin under construction (*Have Gun Will Travel—Young Gun*)

Middle: The *Fury* cabin

Bottom: The rear of the *Fury* cabin next to the corral, with the barn

This set was built after the *Fury* barn was built (which was in 1955) and first appears in the *Fury* television show in 1956. The front of the set was the main entrance while the rear façade was dressed as a bunkhouse. See **Badman's Country** (1958) for the front and **Five Guns to Tombstone** (1960) for the rear. Apparently destroyed in the 1970 wildfire.

Above: The front of the Midway House (*Have Gun Will Travel—The Lady*)
Below: The location of the house in relation to the *Fury* barn

Above: The rear of the house (**Five Guns to Tombstone** 1950)
Below: Wanted Dead or Alive—Eager Man

There were two main cabin sets on the Upper Iverson: the Stone Cabin which first appeared in 1944 and may have been the same building as was in the Gorge until 1944. The other set was the Miner's Cabin, but I prefer to call it the Lone Ranger's Cabin because his hidden silver mine was located underneath the floor of the cabin. This set was in place by 1943.

The Stone Cabin
Below: **Batman and Robin** (1949)

Above: The Lone Ranger/Miner's Cabin
Below: The two fake mine entrances located just to the left of the
Miner's Cabin

UPPER IVERSON — WESTERN TOWN

The final set on the Upper Iverson was a western town/village set located in the northwest corner of the property. It is not seen in a 1956 aerial photograph of the ranch, but does appear in the 1958 aerial. The set, comprising about 10 or 11 buildings, was still in place in 1968, so it was probably destroyed by the September 1970 Newhall-Malibu wildfire which swept through the area. Except for a glimpse of a portion of one building from a distance, I have not been able to located any movie or television show which used the set.

A Glimpse of the Upper Iverson Western Town/Village

Have Gun Will Travel—
The Sons of Aaron Murdock

UPPER IVERSON — FERN ANN BRIDGE, POND, AND CREEK

Located on the southern edge of the main Upper Iverson upper landscape, was a lake which appeared in some films and was missing in others. The original bridge across Fern Ann Creek when Frank Raposo first owned the property, had the ability to be closed, allowing a pond or lake to be created behind it. The stone bottomed Fern Ann Creek bed also appeared in films.

Above: The Fern Ann Creek Bridge
Bottom: A closeup of the opening for creek water to flow through

Top: A good glimpse of the opening in the bridge (**Bonanza Town** 1951)
Above: A closeup view of the valve which closed up the opening in the bridge, creating a dam (**Bonanza Town** 1951)

Two views of the pond/lake
(*The Roy Rogers Show—*
Carnival Killer)

Tarzan and the Slave Girl (1950)
The stone bottomed Fern Ann Creek bed

ACCIDENTS

It is not unusual for accidents to occur on a movie set, especially on location. The Iverson Ranch was no different. We present just a few of those which were reported in newspapers of the time.

In the November 24, 1932, issue of *The Los Angeles Times*, it was reported that A. H. Tanguay, San Fernando Valley publicist and cameraman, "while photographing nineteen lions in a group at the Paramount Publix location on Iverson ranch, came near losing his eyesight when his camera exploded as a result of the sun focusing on the camera lense and blowing up the nitrate film pack within the machine." Luckily, he had been looking at the lions and not into his camera when it exploded. Not stated in the article was the name of the film: **King of the Jungle** with Buster Crabbe.

In the February 18, 1937, issue of *The Van Nuys News*, "Death rode with a Fox Studio bus ... enroute to the Iverson ranch ... and selected as its victim George Hassell ..." Apparently, Hassell was sitting on the front seat next to the bus driver and when they reached their filming location, the driver couldn't awaken Hassell. A doctor was summoned and it was determined that Hassell was dead. The shoot, not mentioned in the article, was **Wee Willie Winkie** with Shirley Temple.

The July 20, 1939, issue of the *Santa Ana Register*, stated that "Monte Blue, veteran actor, was reported resting easily today in Hollywood hospital, where he was treated for several broken ribs and multiple contusions, caused by an unruly horse. Blue was thrown and trampled while riding before the cameras in location scenes of "Geronomo," [sic] being shot at the Iverson ranch."

Tragedy struck a young Van Nuys boy as reported June 30, 1943, *The Los Angeles Times*: "Six-year-old Dennis Joseph Inman ... was drowned yesterday in a ranch lake near Chatsworth when a canoe tipped over. The mishap occurred at the Iverson ranch ... where Dennis had gone with his mother to visit his elder brother, who was working in a film."

The Signal (Newhall, California), November 27, 1947: "A queer case came to light last week when Deputies ... were called to the Iverson Ranch ... to investigate a young transient who had been given shelter there by the owner. Mr. Iverson told the officers that the man gave his name as Hugh Albert Weber, and after being told he could stay at the ranch for a few days, began boasting about shooting a man in Texas. He also complained of his leg hurting him. When Mrs. Iverson investigated she found a wound that looked like a bullet hole, which had become maggot infested."

Shamokin News Dispatch (Shamokin, Pennsylvania) October 1, 1948: "Jeffrey Lynn ... wound up with a cut hand, a wrenched shoulder and a general assortment of head bruises ... Jeff picked up the injuries when Duryea, playing the famouns highwayman [**Black Bart**, Universal], shoved a Wells Fargo driver off a stagecoach onto Lynn."

Death nearly claimed actor Duncan Renaldo when he fractured his neck during filming of the *Cisco Kid* television show. "The accident occurred yesterday at Iverson's ranch in the San Fernando valley when Renaldo was hit by an artificial rock pushed off a cliff by one of the movie villains." [*The Honolulu Advertiser*, June 7, 1953]

Oakland Tribune, July 17, 1953: "From his wire-rigged bed at Hollywood's Cedar of Lebanon hospital, where he [Duncan Renaldo] is recovering from a broken neck, "Cisco" will soon have the dubious pleasure of following a plunge of the studio "rock" that, on June 5th, put him where he is today. Viewers can watch too. The actual footage showing his near-fatal accident while on location at Iverson's Ranch will be seen in a special 55-second insert of a forthcoming "Cisco Kid" episode. It will show a villain rolling a 65-pound papier mache "boulder" off a cliff during the filming. The boulder, which was supposed to miss Renaldo, struck him on the head, breaking his neck. Convalescing slowly, he expects to be back in the saddle in about 10 weeks. KRON will televise this "Cisco Kid" chapter containing the rock sequence either next Thursday (7 p.m.) or the week following, depending on film delivery."

"Actor George Montgomery, ... suffered a deep hand gash Tuesday when he grabbed a knife that took a wrong flip during the filming of a picture. Fifteen stitches were taken in his hand ..." [*Great Falls Tribune* (Great Falls, Montana), June 20, 1956]

STONEY POINT

Stoney Point is a rocky hill formation in the northwest section of Chatsworth. Prior to the Simi Valley Freeway, it was located just east of Santa Susana Pass Road. Now, with the Topanga Canyon Blvd extension, it is located just east of that roadway. It is seen in the background of many scenes filmed at the Iverson Movie Ranch. It is not part of the movie ranch, but is seen many times in film clips and television shows.

The Grapes of Wrath (1940)

Riding Wild (1935)

Facing Page Top: **Superman** (1948)
Facing Page Bottom: The Texan—Dishonest Posse

Publicity Still of Lash LaRue with Stoney Point in the background

OTHER MOVIE SETS AND NON-SETS

Besides the movie sets which stood for several years (see Movie Sets), there were other sets which were built for a single film/television show and then removed, or remained only for a short period of time. Also, on a very few occasions, a real ranch building was used or was seen from a distance.

Above: A movie set built for an unidentified film

Above: A short-lived set at the Garden of the Gods
(**Song of the Saddle** 1936)

Below: A short-lived set on the Upper Iverson
(*Have Gun Will Travel—Fight At Adobe Wells*)

Above: Another short-lived set on the Cliff Road
on the Lower Iverson (*The Lone Ranger—Sheep Thieves*)

Below: This short-lived set appeared in
Have Gun Will Travel—The Prophet

LOWER IVERSON—AARON IVERSON BARN

Aaron Iverson resided on the Lower Iverson. His barn appeared in at least one film, up close, and in several others in the background of shots.

This upclose use of the Aaron Iverson barn is from the
1947 film **Border Feud**.

Above: The barn is on the left (*The Virginian—Strangers at Sundown*)

Below: The barn can be seen above the car (**Superman** 1948)
The barn also appears in **Batman and Robin**.

LOWER IVERSON—THE OLD FOLKS HOME

In 1927, Charles (Karl) and Agusta Iverson built a home on the cliff to the south of the Indian Hills area, overlooking Chatsworth and the San Fernando Valley. It was referred to as "The Old Folks Home". It appeared, partially, in at least one film, and has been seen in the background (by accident) of television shows such as *The Life and Legend of Wyatt Earp.*

The Old Folks Home under construction circa 1927

Above: The Old Folks Home in January 1930

Below: A scene from **Outlaw Deputy** 1935

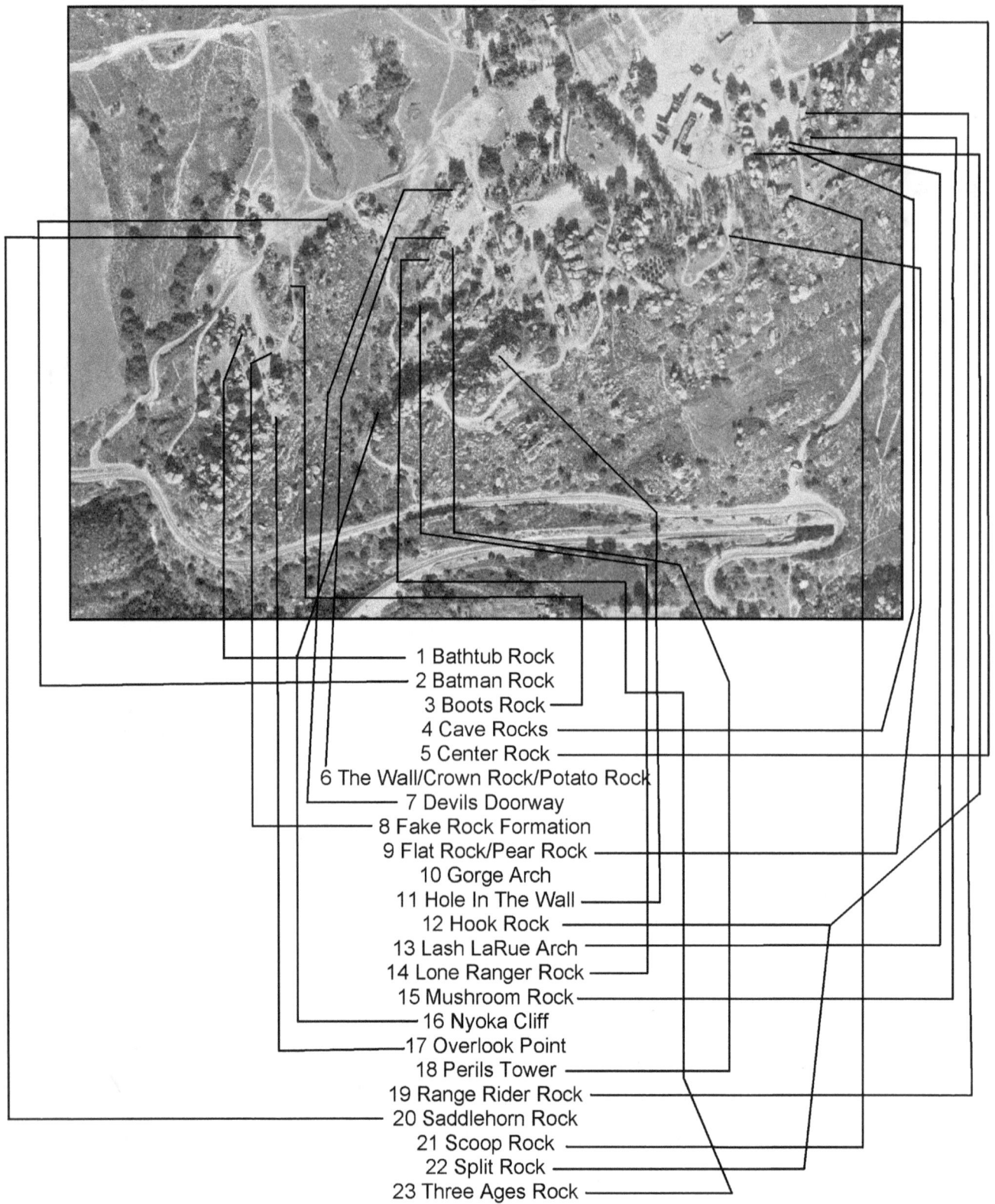

1 Bathtub Rock
2 Batman Rock
3 Boots Rock
4 Cave Rocks
5 Center Rock
6 The Wall/Crown Rock/Potato Rock
7 Devils Doorway
8 Fake Rock Formation
9 Flat Rock/Pear Rock
10 Gorge Arch
11 Hole In The Wall
12 Hook Rock
13 Lash LaRue Arch
14 Lone Ranger Rock
15 Mushroom Rock
16 Nyoka Cliff
17 Overlook Point
18 Perils Tower
19 Range Rider Rock
20 Saddlehorn Rock
21 Scoop Rock
22 Split Rock
23 Three Ages Rock

THE ROCKS

The rock formations at the Iverson Movie Ranch were in a class of their own, almost as important as the films shot there or the stars who appeared in them. This section of the book will look at many of the major rock formations, as this is one aspect of the ranch which is pretty unique—the rocks have been given names!

The Garden of the Gods
(see Garden of the Gods section)

Three Ages (1923)
Buster Keaton

Batman and Robin (1949)

Above: Unidentified Charles Starrett Western
Below: **Come On Leathernecks** (1938)

Above: **Perils of Nyoka** (1942)
Below: **Riding With Buffalo Bill** (1954)

Above: **Rocky Mountain Rangers** (1940)
Below: **Batman and Robin** (1949)

Above: **Tarzan the Ape Man** (1932)

Below: Have Gun Will Travel—The Yuma Treasure

Above: Potato Rock/The Wall in
The Charge of the Light Brigade (1936)

Below: Crown Rock in **The Big Show** (1936)

Above: **Oh Susanna!** (1936) looking southerly
Below: **Oh Susanna!** (1936) looking northerly

Above: Visitors to the fake rock house
Below: **Three Ages** (1923)

Above: **Man, Woman, Marriage** (1920)
Rock House is on far left

Below: **Tell It to the Marines** (1926)
Rock House is on left side

Above: Flat Rock and Pear Rock

Below: **Wee Willie Winkie** (1937)
Flat Rock is on the left and Pear Rock on the right

Above: **Bells of Rosarita** (1945)
Pear Rock

Below: **The Three Stooges Meet Hercules** (1962)
Flat Rock

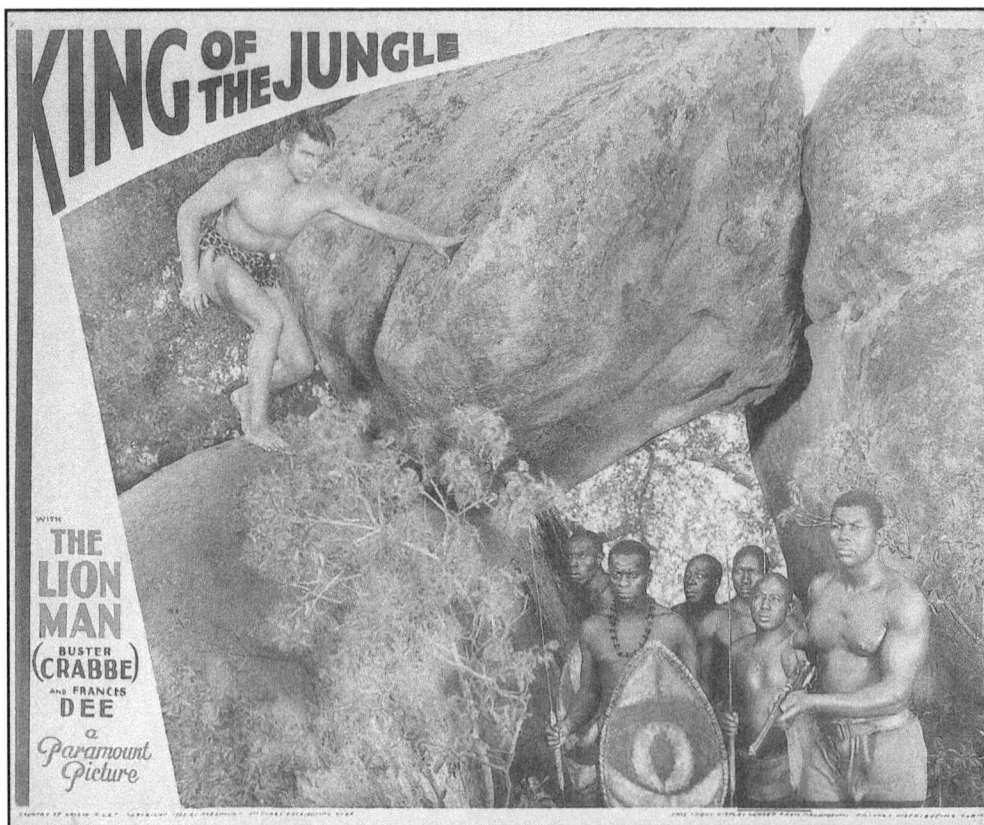

Above: **King of the Jungle** (1933)
Below: Have Gun Will Travel—A Snare For Murder

Above: **King of the Texas Rangers** (1941)
Below: **Marshal of Heldorado** (1950)

Above: **California Mail** (1936)
Below: **Trailin' West** (1936)

The Phantom Rider (1946)
Hook Rock is is near the middle of the image

Above: **King of the Bullwhip** (1950) Publicity Still

Above: The Lone Ranger (1957)
Below: Ben-Hur (1925)

Above: **Man From Colorado** (1941)
Mushroom Rock center right; saucer rock on left
Below: Have Gun Will Travel—Show of Force

Above: Nyoka climbing up ladder in **Perils of Nyoka** (1942)

Below: On top of Nyoka Cliff, **Perils of Nyoka** (1942)

Above: **Rimfire** (1949)
Below: **The Real Glory** (1939)—on top of Nyoka Cliff

Above: **Adventures of Marco Polo** (1938)
Below: **Gunmen of Abilene** (1950)
Overlook Point on left of Rocky's shoulder

Above: Perils Tower on right—**Perils of Nyoka** (1942)
Below: **Perils of Nyoka** (1942)—closer view of Perils Tower

Above: Annie Oakley—Annie and the Six O'Spades
Below: **Shut My Big Mouth** (1942)

Superman (1948)

Young Daniel Boone (1950)

Top: Wyatt Earp—Three (Scopp Rock on left side)
Bottom: Bonanza—My Brother's Keeper

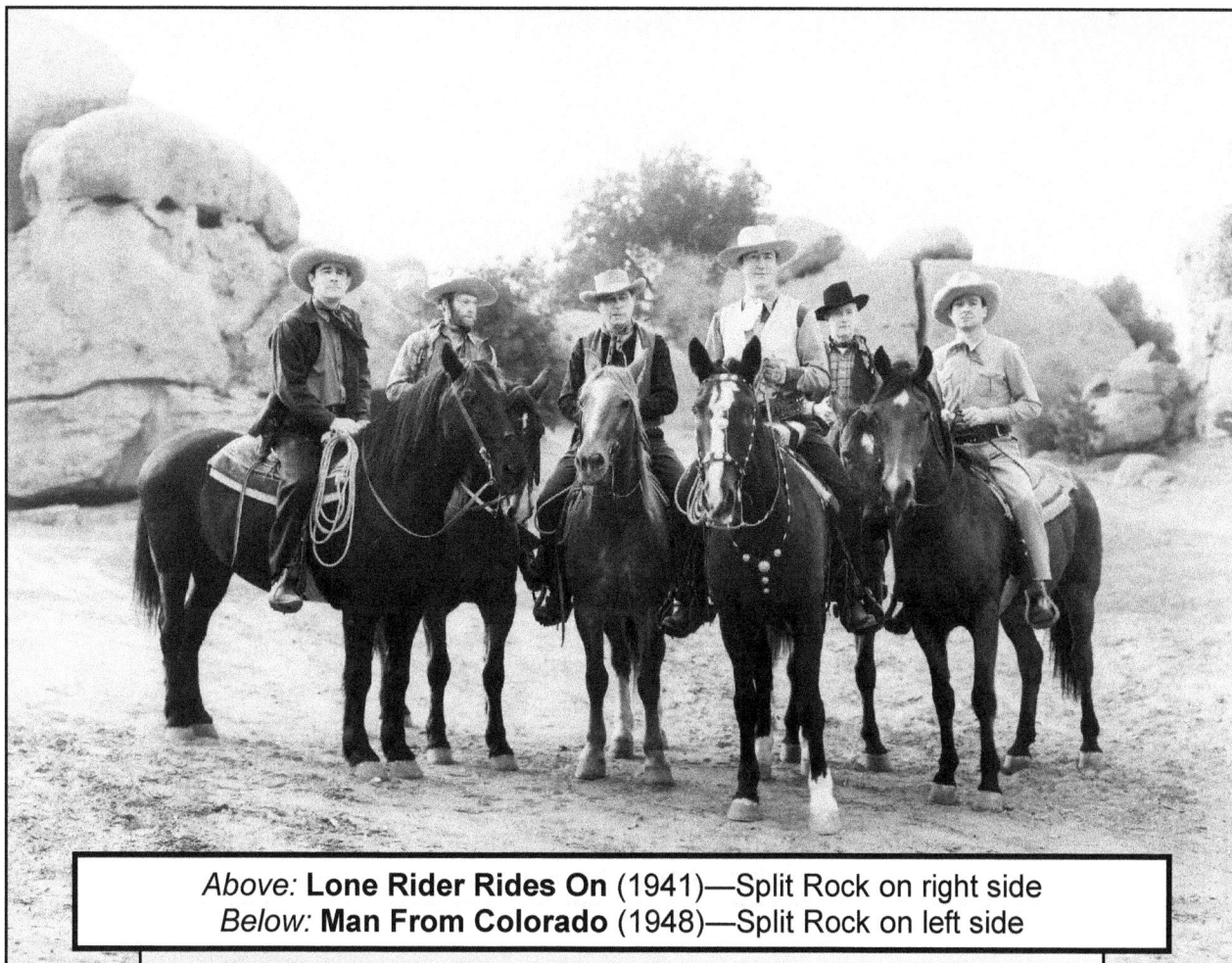

Above: **Lone Rider Rides On** (1941)—Split Rock on right side
Below: **Man From Colorado** (1948)—Split Rock on left side

Above: **Charge of the Light Brigade** (1936)
Below: **Three Ages** (1923)

Above: **King of the Jungle** (1933)
Below: **Tarzan the Ape Man** (1932)

A 1948 photograph of Ambush Pass

Above: Have Gun Will Travel—The Chase
Below: Annie Oakley—Annie's Desert Adventure

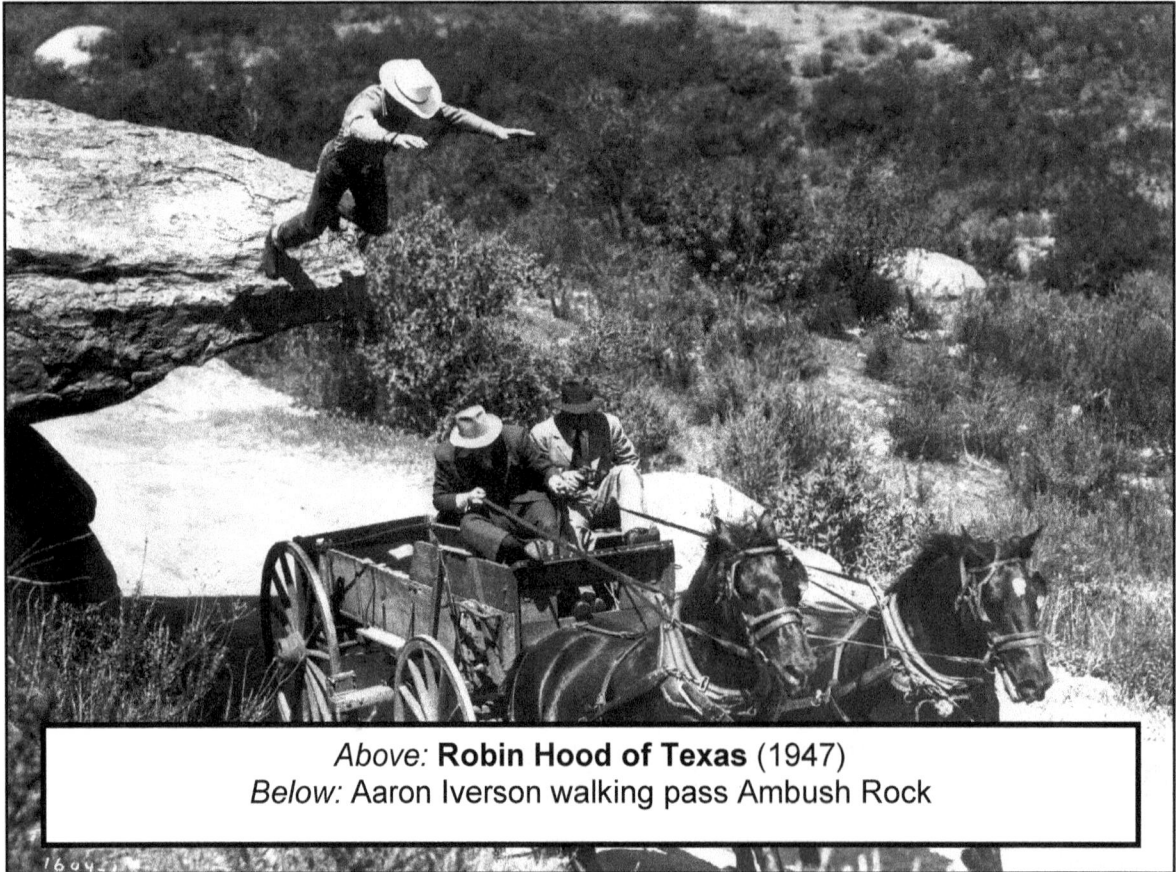

Above: **Robin Hood of Texas** (1947)
Below: Aaron Iverson walking pass Ambush Rock

Above: **Riders in the Sky** (1949)

Below: The Gene Autry Show—Stage to San Dimas

Above: **Overland Stage Raiders** (1938)
Eagle Beak is between John Wayne and Max Terhune
Below: **Bonanza Town** (1951)

The Maverick (1952)
These rocks are in the northwest section of the Upper Iverson. The Upper Iverson Western Town was built behind this rock formation.

Above: Frontier Doctor—Crooked Circle
Below: **Snake River Desperadoes** (1951)
A view of the northwest Upper Iverson, northeast Brandeis Ranch,
and Fern Ann Springs

Above: **Daredevils of the West** (1943)
Below: **Grandpa Goes to Town** (1949)

Above: **Zorro's Fighting Legion** (1939)
Below: **Prairie Pioneers** (1941)

Above: **Ghost Town Renegades** (1947)
Below: **Frisco Tornado** (1950)

Above: The Totem Pole Rocks

Below: **Tarzan and the Slave Girl** (1950)

Perils of Nyoka (1942)

Above: Whale Rock
Below: **Boots Malone** (1952)

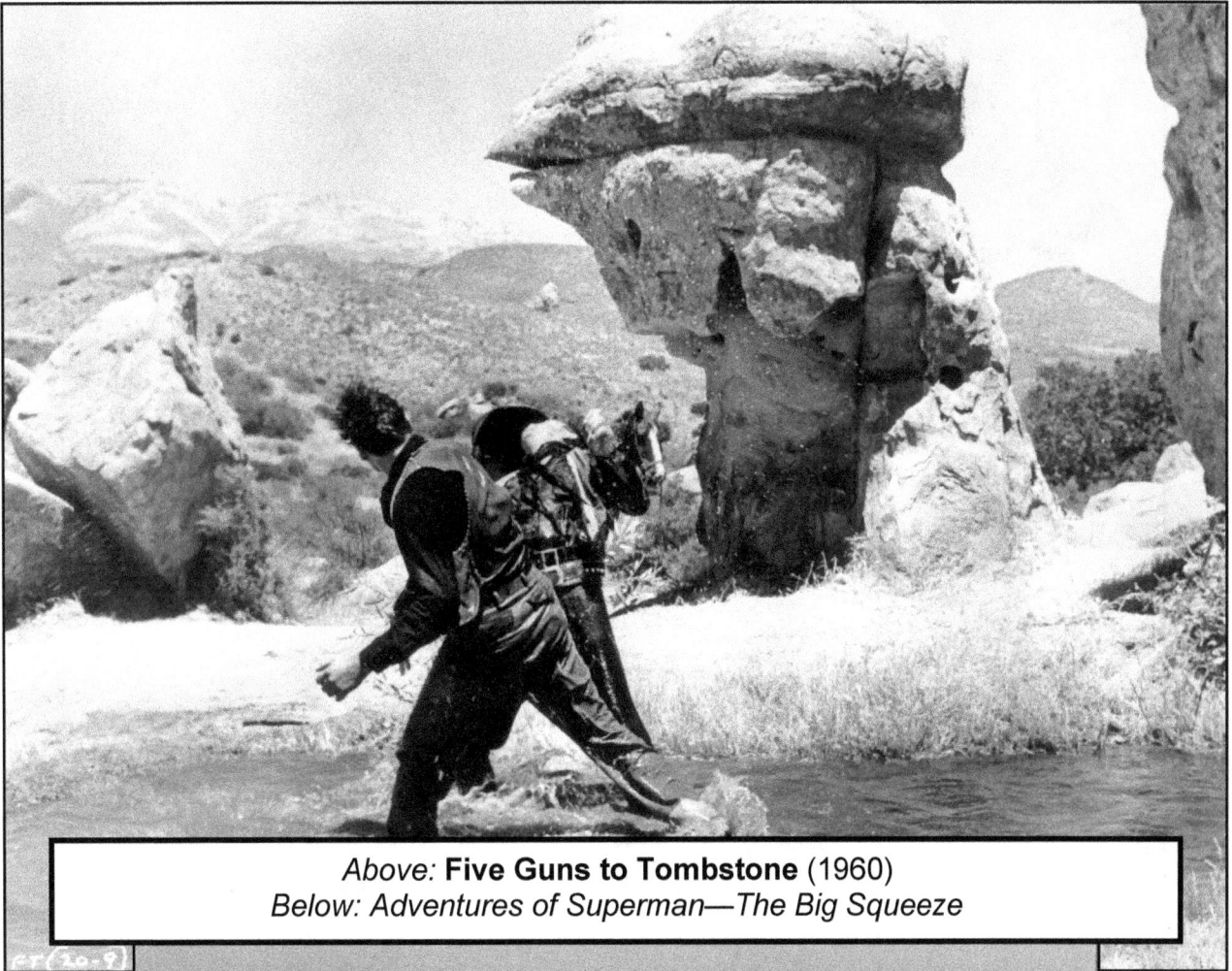

Above: **Five Guns to Tombstone** (1960)
Below: Adventures of Superman—The Big Squeeze

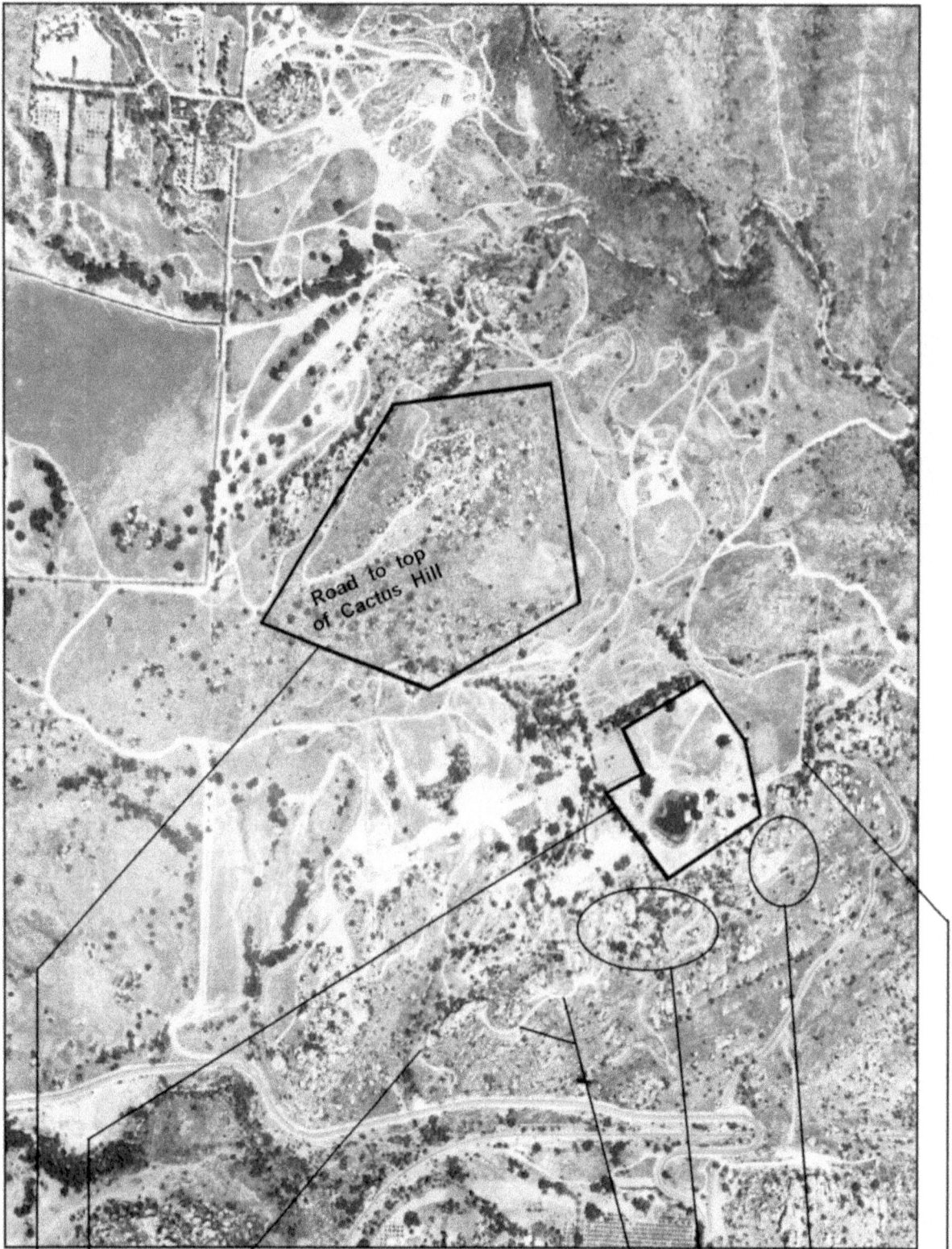

Road to top of Cactus Hill

1960 Aerial Photograph

Sheep Flats

Cactus Hill
Cliff Road

Silverland
East Gate
Indian Hills
Steep Canyon Road

MISCELLANEOUS FEATURES OF THE RANCH

Besides movie sets, besides beautiful rock formations, there were other features of the ranch which will be mentioned in this section which do not fit into other parts of this book (see map on facing page).

Sheep Flats—An area of the ranch of mostly flat land located just east of the homes of Aaron and Joseph Iverson. It became the area where the **Wee Willie Winkie** and **Along Came Jones** sets were built, later becoming a trailer park.

Cactus Hill—This was and is the large hill of the Upper Iverson running from the border with the Lower Iverson (now the Simi Valley Freeway) northward. The northwestern and northern side of the hill was filled with rock formations (see the Rocks Section). The rocks were used a lot for filming while most of the rest of the hill was left alone. One or two films may have been shot up on top. On the western side of the hill was a road running up from the Upper Iverson insert road area (the western side of the Upper Iverson next to the Brandeis Ranch) to the top of the hill.

Cliff Road—Also known as the Stagecoach Road, it ran around the base of Nyoka Cliff.

Steep Canyon Road—Another road built for filming to the east of Nyoka Cliff at the top level of those hills between Nyoka Cliff and the Indian Hills area.

Indian Hills—Located immediately south of Sheep Flats. A few sets and the Old Folks Home were located there.

Silverland—An area just behind the rocks on the southeast side of Sheep Flats. The Iverson property continued eastward from there to the old Mayan Drive (prior to freeway construction and the Topanga Canyon Blvd extension).

East Gate—While the main entrance to the ranch was off of Santa Susana Pass Road on the southwestern side of the ranch, the east side of the ranch was accessible through this gate via Mayan Drive. Just on the other side of Mayan Drive was the county fire station for the area (moved because of the freeway construction and Topanga Canyon Blvd extension).

Above: The Road Up Cactus Hill seen here in **Crooked River** (1950)
appeared in a few films including **Perils of Nyoka** (1942)

Below: The Steep Canyon Road/Stagecoach Road
as seen in **Crooked River** (1950)

Joe Iverson working on the Steep Canyon Road

CLIFF ROAD—Built on the top of a hill in the Indian Hills area, it ran from near the Old Folks Home, along the cliff overlooking Chatsworth, around through the pass which fronted on the Vultura Palace, then back uphill (circular in general nature).

Above: **Batman and Robin** (1949)

Below: **Daredevils of the West** (1943)

Perils of Nyoka (1942)

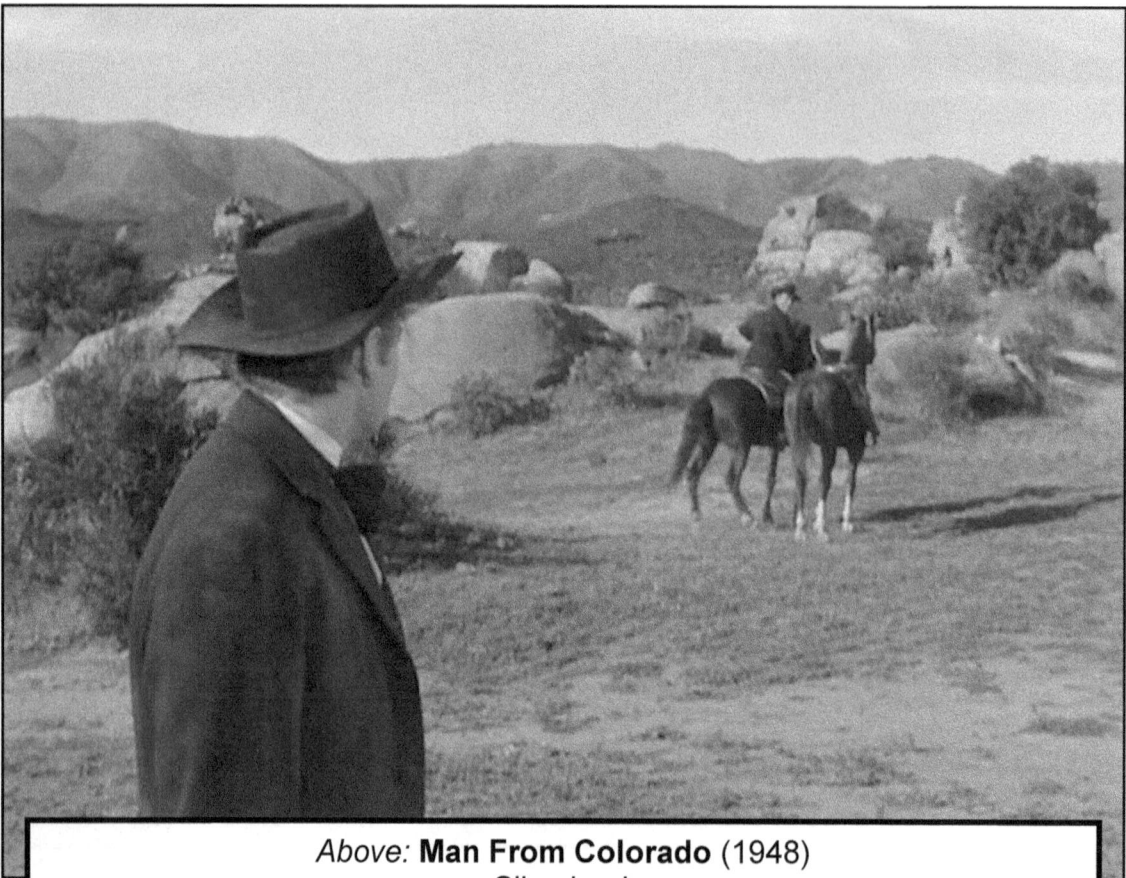

Above: **Man From Colorado** (1948)
Silverland
Below: **Perils of Nyoka** (1942)

Above: **Perils of Nyoka** (1942)
Silverland
Below: The Lone Ranger—The Lone Ranger Finds Silver

The Lone Ranger—The Lone Ranger Finds Silver

Silverland

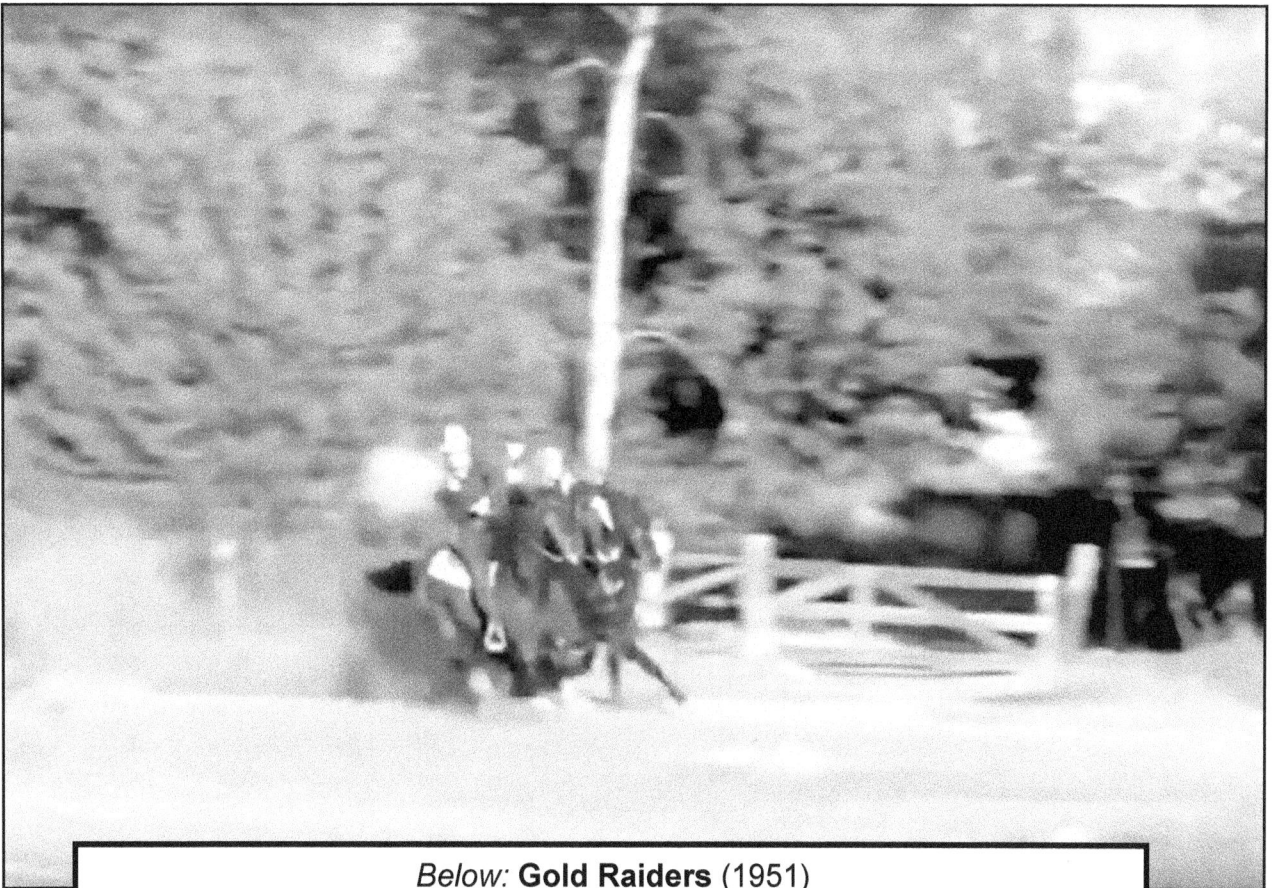

Below: **Gold Raiders** (1951)
East Gate
Below: The Rifleman—First Wages

The train route heading south from the Iverson Movie Ranch—
seen in many films, usually in stock footage

TRAINS

Just south of the main Lower Iverson Ranch land is Santa Susana Pass Road. Running along on the south side of that is a portion of the Southern Pacific Railroad line which runs from Chatsworth to Simi Valley (exiting the last tunnel next to Corriganville). A portion of the train line next to Santa Susana Pass Road just west of Topanga Canyon Blvd. is right-of-way which the S.P. Railroad purchased from the Iverson's back in 1902. Santa Susana Pass Road through that same area also was purchased from the Iverson's. While both routes (train and roadway) were originally part of the Iverson Ranch, we will not consider the films which were shot on them as part of the history of the ranch, except for one film which used a portion of original homestead land just to the south and east of the train tracks (**The Garden of Allah**).

The Garden of Allah (1936)
Looking south, set built just south and east of the train tracks

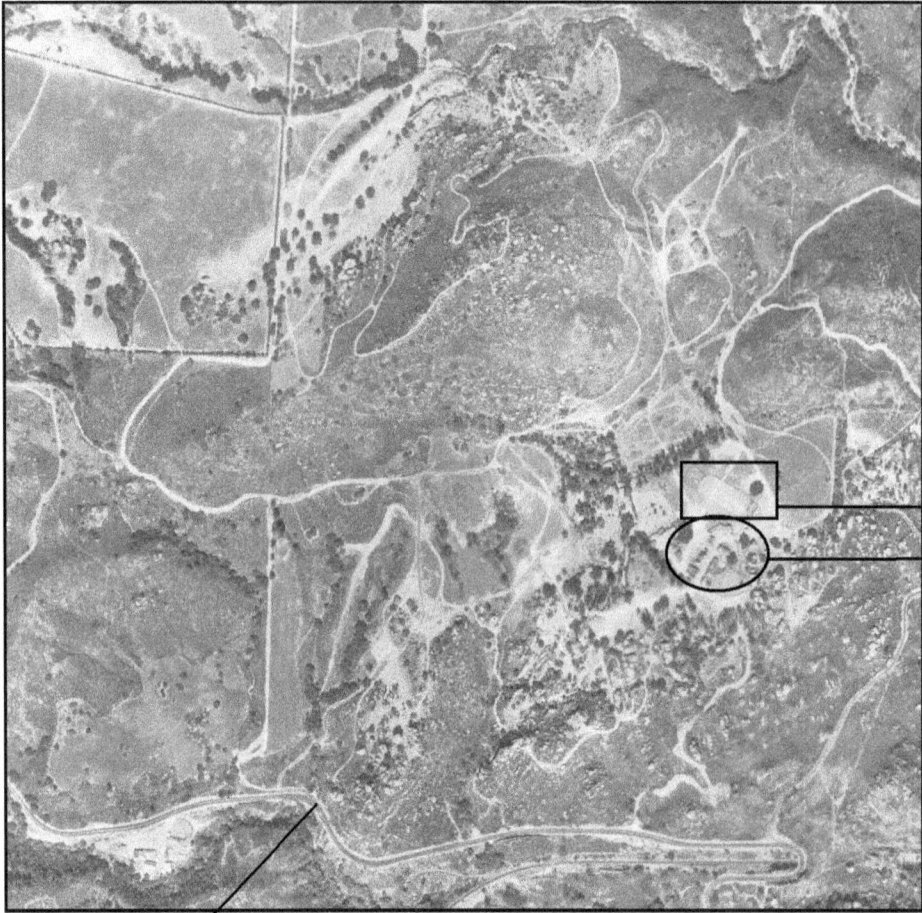

Iverson Ranch in 1954

Western Street Set ——————————————————

Rodeo Arena ——————————————————————

—— Santa Susana Pass Road

RODEO ROUNDUP

First appearing in the June 1, 1953, issue of *Broadcasting Telecasting* magazine as well as in the May 28, 1953, issue of *The San Bernardino County Sun* and the May 30, 1953, issue of the *Long Beach Independent* newspapers, it was announced that the Los Angeles television station KNBH (now KNBC) channel 4 would begin broadcasting "Rodeo Roundup" on Saturday, May 30, 1953 from 4:30 pm to 5:30 pm. The show would originate from the Iverson Ranch where a rodeo arena with seating accomodating 5,000 spectators, and stock pens for more than 200 steers, Brahma bulls and calves were erected. In addition to the major rodeo events, calf roping, bronc riding, bull riding and bull dogging, the telecast would include shooting, roping and whip exhibitions from the adjacent western set.

The show was hosted by Cowboy Slim, the 1950 bulldogging champion of the association. The rodeo was held under the rules of the Cowboy Association of America. Between 150 and 200 cowboys participated each week.

The June 6th episode featured Miss Edie Moore of Long Beach in the calf roping contest. Also on that episode was the Indian village which was set up at Roundup Town (the Iverson western street set) by "White Cloud and his tribe of real Indians" (*Long Beach Independent*, June 6, 1953).

The June 20th episode include a wedding. "Wedding on horseback will be novel feature of Cowboy Slim's Rodeo Roundup Town Sunday at Iverson's Ranch in Chatsworth. The ceremony in the arena will take place just before the C.A.A. rodeo show starting at 2:30 p.m. The event will be open to the public. Grace Pickerell, the bride-to-be, will come down the aisle in a stage coach. Bridegroom Bill Chaney, Hollywood stunt man, will await on horseback with his best man, Cowboy Slim. Rev. Carl E. Burns, on a white horse, will perform the nuptials. Motion picture and television stars are expected to attend the ceremony." (*The Van Nuys News*, June 14, 1953)

The rodeo arena, as can be seen in the aerial photograph from 1954, was directly adjacent on the north side of the western street set built by Gary Cooper for **Along Came Jones** in 1945. Unfortunately, so far, I have been unable to unearth any photographs or video footage of the television show. After eight episodes on the air, the show was transferred to Crash Corrigan's Corriganville Ranch (beginning on July 25, 1953).

A slight glimpse of a portion of the arena can be seen in the 1957 episode "Tuffy" of the *Annie Oakley Show*. Also, a small glimpse is also seen in *Sky King* in an unnamed episode from 1955.

By 1958, as seen in the aerial photograph, not only is the western street gone but also the rodeo arena. In a few more years, this portion of the ranch would be sold off to become a mobile home/trailer park.

Aerial view of the western street in 1955. A small section of the rodeo arena fencing can be seen in the lower right corner. From *Sky King* television show.

Looking north at the Casa Grande falsefront on the western street in 1957 as seen in "Tuffy" episode of *Annie Oakley*. A part of the rodeo arena fencing can be seen to the right of the Casa Grande set.

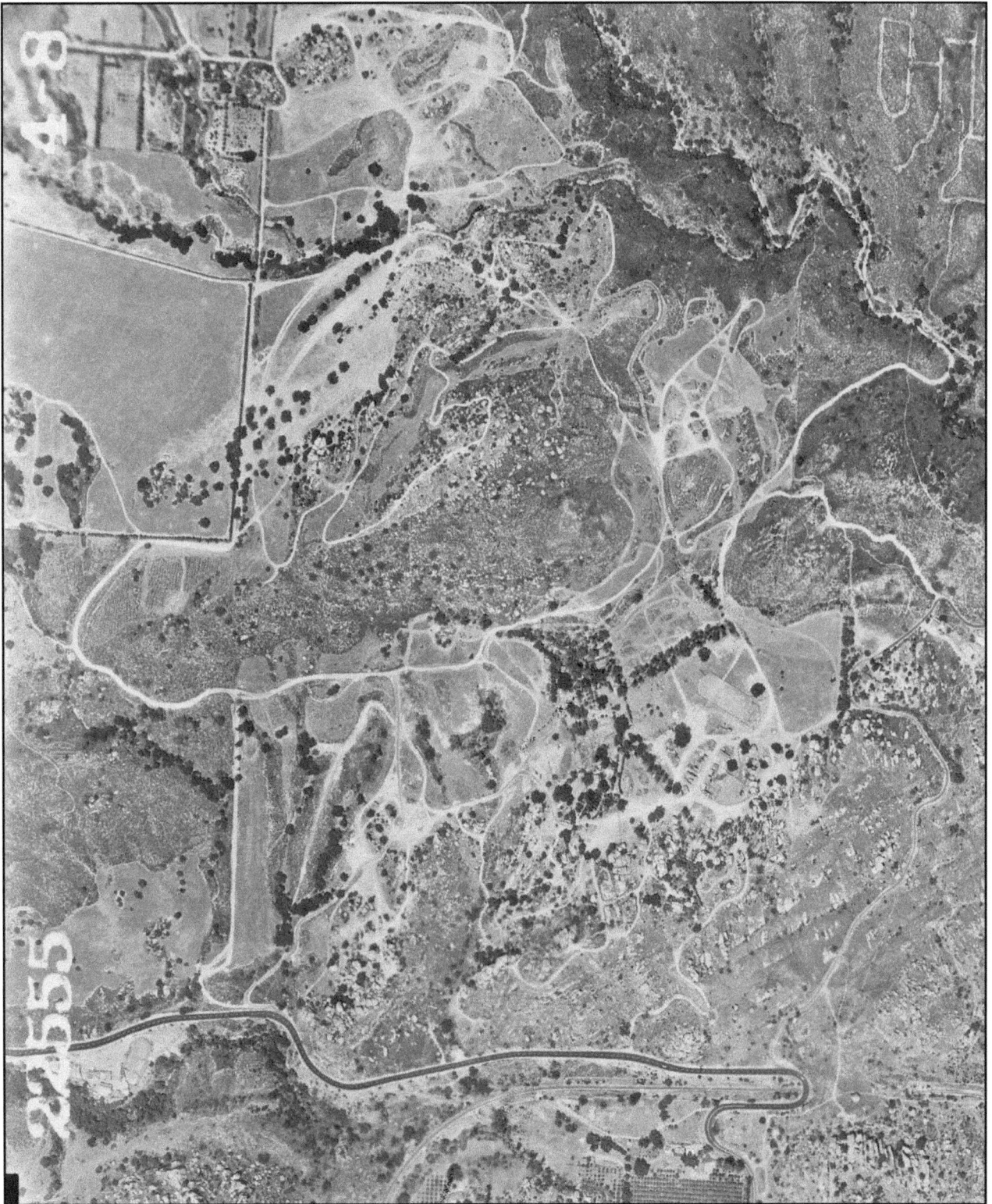

1956 aerial photograph of the Iverson Movie Ranch
The rodeo arena is still visible (middle right) and
the western street is still there
(decaying and soon to be removed)

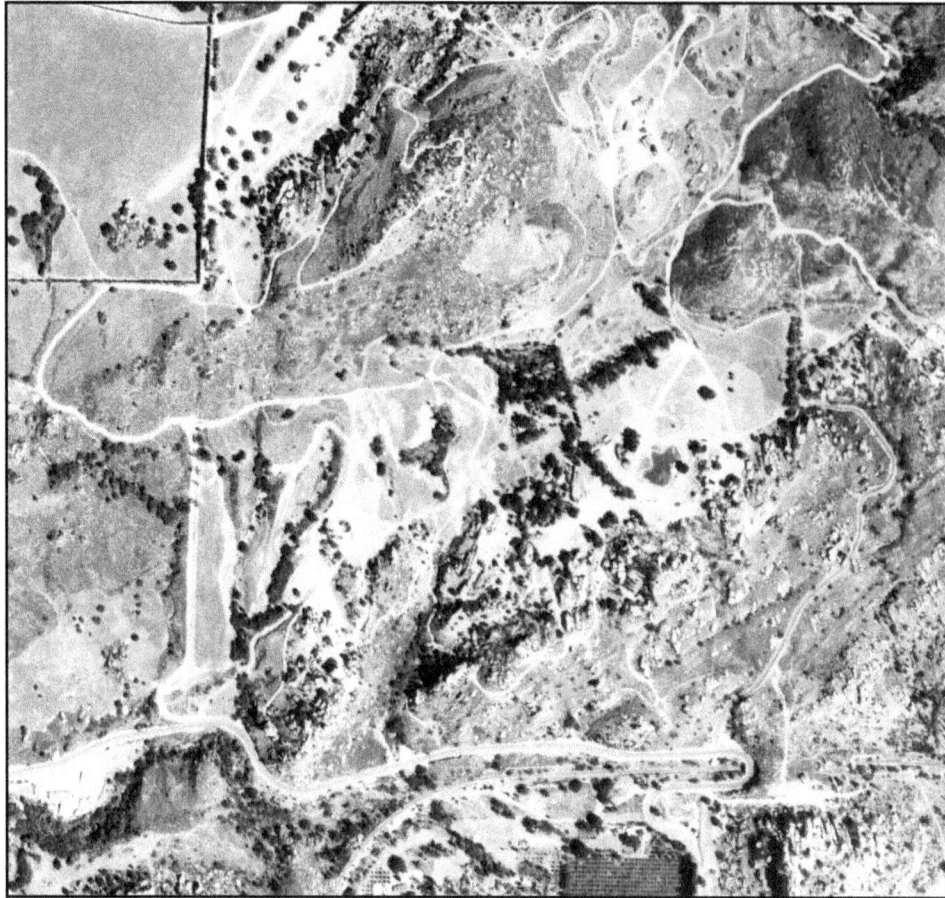

1958 aerial photograph of the Iverson Movie Ranch
Western town set and rodeo arena have been removed
and a small lake now sits in the area of the town

THE BEGINNING OF THE END

With the death of their parents, the two remaining owners of the Iverson Movie Ranch, Aaron Ephraim and Joseph Adolph, took over the complete reins of operating the historic movie ranch. Aaron became owner of the Upper Iverson while Joseph controlled the Lower Iverson, and they operated the entire ranch as a joint venture.

While the 1950s kept the ranch busy with movies, television shows, and photo shoots, the brothers were soon to find out that the usefulness and life of the ranch would be severely limited when they were told of the impending construction of the 118 Freeway (aka Simi Valley/Ronald Reagan) which would run through the northern section of the Lower Iverson, cutting the ranch in half.

With the knowledge of the upcoming construction of the freeway, the brothers allowed the movie sets which sat in the freeway's path to deterioate. The remaining buildings of the **Wee Willie Winkie** set and the western town built for **Along Came Jones** were the first casualties of the future freeway. The western town was completely removed by 1958 and a lot of the Indian set was also gone by then, with the remaining buildings gone in 1963 when 17.5 acres of the Sheep Flats section of the ranch was put up for sale and soon became the Indian Hills Mobile Home Village, then located at 21885 Mayan Drive, later Topanga Canyon Blvd.

Between 1956 and 1958, a small western town set was built at the northwest section of the Upper Iverson, added to the already built Fury Set and the Midway House in the middle of the Upper Iverson (see their histories in the Movie Sets section).

A September 1970 wildfire destroyed virtually all of the movie sets on the ranch which were still standing.

Above: Freeway under construction in 1968
Below: Freeway finished in 1971

THE FREEWAY

The local area newspapers mentioned the Simi Valley Freeway in the August 8, 1958, issue of *The Los Angeles Times* and was again mentioned the following year on March 29, 1959, *The Los Angeles Times*. On July 21, 1960, *The Los Angeles Times* reported that "[State Sen. Robert J. Lagomarsino] said he believes the earlier 1965 starting date was moved up as a result of appeals for an accelerated construction schedule."

The Van Nuys News, March 1, 1964: "A Planning Dept. report explains preliminary plans for the north extension of Topanga Canyon Blvd. to the Simi Valley Freeway, as prepared by the State Division of Highways, indicate the boulevard grade would bring it from two to seven feet above the present ground level at the proposed Valley Circle Blvd. intersection." Up to that point in time, Topanga Canyon Blvd stopped at Devonshire Street. Santa Susana Pass Road then continued northward until it headed off westerly. With the building of the freeway north of Santa Susana Pass Road, it was decided to extend Topanga Canyon Blvd all of the way to the freeway, cutting through the Silverland area on the eastern side of the Iverson Ranch.

The Los Angeles Times, April 5, 1966: "The State Division of Highways ... has awarded a $14.4 million contract for construction of the first mile segment of the Simi Freeway. ... Successful bidder was the Kirst Construction Co. of Altadena ..."

The Los Angeles Times, April 20, 1966: "Actual work on the Simi Freeway began with clearing of trees and stumps last week along Topanga Canyon Blvd. north from Devonshire St. in Chatsworth."

The Los Angeles Times, August 29, 1966: "When completed in another two years, the freeway will bypass congested Santa Susana Pass and open the way across the mountains into Ventura County from the West Valley."

Santa Susana Pass Road continued to be in its original alignment from 1966 until sometime around 1991 when an extension was built to connect it directly with Topanga Canyon Blvd instead of its more leisurely route. The old section which was blocked off was renamed Old Santa Susana Pass Road and is used only for local traffic.

Prior to the construction of the freeway and the extension of Topanga Canyon Blvd, the eastern side of the Iverson Ranch, Twin Lakes, the Indian Hills Mobile Home Village, and the L. A. County Fire Station No. 75 were accessed via Mayan Drive. Portions of that roadway can still be found, but the Topanga Canyon Blvd extension runs right through most of the area it used to be located on.

Top Left: Los Angeles Times, August 27, 1967
Top Right: The Van Nuys News, June 18, 1970
Bottom Left: The Los Angeles Times, June 7, 1970

176

THE END

The end of the Iverson Movie Ranch under the ownership of the Iverson family began in late August 1967 when Aaron Iverson put up for sale 93.5 acres of the Upper Iverson. Three years later, in June 1970, with the dissolution of the joint venture between Aaron and Joseph Iverson to run the Iverson Movie Ranch, 213 acres of the Lower Iverson plus 442 acres of the rest of the Iverson Ranch were put up for sale through auction with the Marsh Dozar company of Beverly Hills. In August 1973, the 213 acres of the Lower Iverson were put up for sale again through a foreclosure sale. Apparently Henry R. Steele became the new owner of the Lower Iverson property which had been sold off. At least 30 acres of the original homestead area had not been sold off and was still owned by Joseph Iverson and the heirs of Aaron Iverson who had died on May 9, 1973.

The plans which Steele outlined for the Lower Iverson, included a rodeo ground, tennis club, golf course, and miles of equestrian trails. None of that came to fruition and he apparently sold off his holding to the Kaufman and Broad company. This company built the California West 290-unit town home and duplex development on the Lower Iverson in 1987.

In 1986, grading and construction of the Summerset Village, a 280-unit condominium development in the area where the Middle Iverson Ranch Set had once stood (on the southeast section of the Upper Iverson) began.

Around 1984, grading and construction began on the Indian Springs/Indian Falls development on the remaining acreage of the Upper Iverson and the adjoining Brandeis Ranch. This became a gated community.

Robert Sherman, said to be a relative of Joe Iverson's second wife, purchased from Joe the remaining few acres of the Iverson Ranch. In 1997, he directed the final film shot on the original ranch land by a relative of the Iverson's (**Motorcycle Cheerleading Mammas**) and he sold that last piece of movie history to Phyliss Murphy and Van Swearingen, along with the "Iverson Movie Location Ranch" name.

Ronald Reagan, Ann Blyth and John McIntyre appear in a scene from the "Death Valley Days" series. Reagan also filmed "Cattle Queen of Montana" and "Code of the Secret Service" at the Iverson Ranch."

Valley Landmarks

Former homestead film location for Hollywood epics and serials

By JERRY BERNS

The scene of more than 2,000 movies, the Iverson Movie Ranch in Chatsworth is a distinguished landmark on many counts.

The ranch is not only the oldest ranch in the Valley, but the owner, Robert Sherman, claims it is the oldest movie studio in the world.

The story begins in 1882 when Augusta Wagman, Sherman's great, great, great aunt, homesteaded the 160-acre property.

Wagman, who emigrated from Sweden to New York, immediately headed west to live near relatives who had moved to the Valley three years previously.

For six years, Wagman worked the property—which extended to what is now Stoney Point on the east, the Nike base on the north and up to the Ventura Country line—alone. In 1888, she married Karl Iverson.

The Iversons had five children, two sets of fraternal twins —a boy and a girl in each set— and another son.

The youngest son, Joe, was to become the most instrumental figure in the ranch's development into a world-renown movie location.

During 1912, two major events shaped the fate of the Iverson family, Valley history and the Iverson Ranch.

The California Aquaduct was completed, bringing water to the San Fernando Valley and ending the terrible drought that had plagued Chatsworth ranchers and farmers.

Please see IVERSON, Page 37

IVERSON: Scene of classic films to open again as recreation area

Continued from Page 14

In addition, movie moguls were flocking to Hollywood from New York to produce their moving pictures more economically and efficiently.

The main reason for the westward migration of the early movie companies was the everlasting sunshine.

With so much rain and snow in New York, outdoor shooting was many times impossible, especially for the type of movies in vogue at the time—western serials and assorted B movies, most of which consisted of one or two reels.

But there was another advantage to relocating in the Los Angeles area: the terrain was diverse.

Mountains, desert and ocean were located close to each other, and film makers found the Southland ideal for location shooting.

The rugged landscape of the Iverson ranch, surrounded by deep canyons and enormous, jutting boulders, set the perfect stage for a variety of films.

It served as the western town for such movie classics as "Stagecoach" and "The Cisco Kid." It also was the sprawling Ponderosa Ranch on the long-running television series, "Bonanza."

Iverson Ranch was the scene for multitudes of Biblical, historical and fantasy films as well. The chariot races on both versions of "Ben Hur," plus many other scenes from the epic drama, were films at Iverson Ranch.

A spectacular rock formation, dubbed "garden of the gods," worked equally well for such diverse movies as "Noah's Ark," "David and Goliath" and "The Amazonians."

Jungles were created for a host of Tarzan movies, and a Palestinian village was built for the filming of "Wee Willie Winkie," with Shirley Temple.

The diversity of terrain at the ranch proved suitable for diametrically different movies such as "Alice in Wonderland" and "The Grapes of Wrath."

Meanwhile, while several crews were shooting many different movies similtaneously at the ranch, life went on for Augusta and Karl and their family.

They raised cattle, pigs and chickens while clearing the land for crops and citrus orchards, all of which they hauled into surrounding towns to sell.

The boys would hunt small animals for the family to eat. Augusta started a honey business and sold more than two tons a year. She also cultivated a vineyard.

Karl tended crops in other parts of the San Fernando Valley and would leave for up to 30 days at a time. The money that came in from the location shoots supplemented all these ventures.

The heyday for the movie industry at Iverson Ranch was realized in the 1930s, '40s and '50s.

Joe Iverson continued living on the ranch with his folks and fully participated in all the filming by helping to construct sets, repairing roads and sometimes even playing as an extra in some of the movies.

Both Augusta and Karl died in 1948, just months apart. Joe continued the tradition of movie making at the ranch and the filming of television series during the 1950s.

During 1957, portions of 57 episodes were shot at the ranch for such series as "The Lone Ranger" and "The Roy Rogers Show."

During the next year, more than 100 productions were filmed. They included "The Real McCoys," "Sky King" and "Gunsmoke."

Hundreds of movies continued to be filmed until the mid-1970s, when Joe fulfilled his lifelong dream of full-time travel.

Today, new owner Sherman is restoring the ranch to its former condition. He is planning a grand reopening in mid-March to reintroduce the movie studios to the ranch.

The original family home still stands, but verandas have been added.

While most of the land has been sold, there is still 10 acres punctuated by the same boulders seen in hundreds of classic films.

Currently, Sherman rents out the property for special events such as weddings and corporate picnics.

There is enough room to seat 500 people, in addition to providing parking for that number.

Barbecues, a nine-hole putting green, a volleyball court, croquet area, horseshoe pit and badminton court have been added for the enjoyment of guests.

When the renovations are complete, there will be a fully stocked fish pond, an outdoor dance floor, a 7,000-square-foot barbecue area, a stage and observation balconies.

Those who would like to pass along interesting facts about Valley landmarks may call Berns, president of Jerry Berns and Associates Realtors, at (818) 788-0446, or write him at 13756 Ventura Blvd., Sherman Oaks, CA 91423.

Hero Monte Hale, left, and villain, Roy Barcroft, are parted by Indians.

John Wayne, left, staggers from blow by Eddie Parker—always a big scene in a horse opera.

Spending a Day At Horse Opera

● By Merrill Panitt

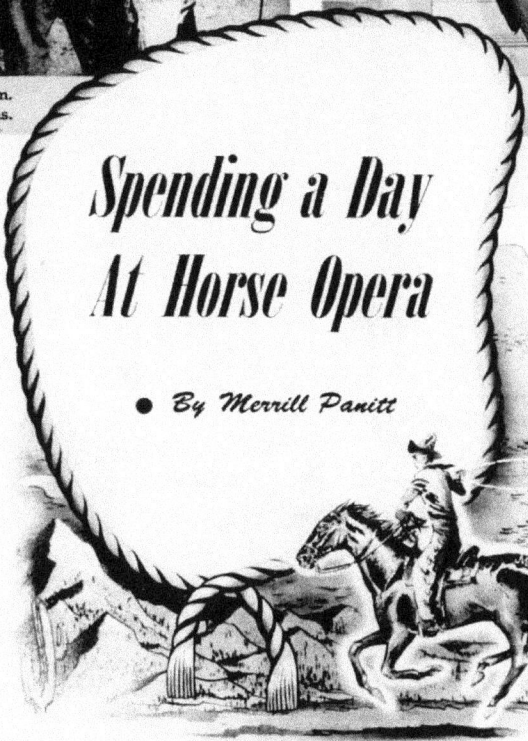

REPUBLIC STUDIOS, home of cowboy epics, revealed recently that Orson Welles, the one-man crowd, would produce, direct and star in a film version of *Macbeth*.

This was not a surprise to Hollywood—it was a thunderbolt. The news was comparable to an announcement from the Acme Button Company saying the company was preparing to manufacture locomotives.

Hedda Hopper gasped. Louella Parsons, who doesn't like Welles anyway, wagged her head.

Jimmy Fidler started composing an open letter to Shakespeare, urging that the script of *Macbeth* be cleaned up before being filmed.

The Johnston office went into a huddle over whether to censor the "damned" in Lady Macbeth's speech about "out damned spot."

Your correspondent rushed out to the Republic lot to find out what had been done with Gene Autry, Roy Rogers, William Elliott, John Wayne, Monte Hale, Allen Lane and other horse opera stars. Were *Trigger, Champion, Pardner* and other horses being put out to pasture, or whatever one does with horses? Would Orson Welles do *Macbeth* on horseback? Would Birnam Wood come to Dunsinane in a covered wagon? Would Macbeth and Macduff fight it out with six-shooters instead of swords? These and many more vital questions troubled us.

IN NO more time than it takes to say, "Smile when you say that, stranger," we were put at ease. Carefully and deliberately the publicity people explained that the Welles *Macbeth* would be performed as written—without cowboy influence. It was pointed out, additionally, that because of competition under new rules for releasing pictures, Republic already had launched a program calling for many million dollar productions each year.

"Does this," we asked, a catch in our voice, "mean the end of cowboy pictures?"

It does not. Be reassured, friends. Life is worth living. Virtue will continue to reign triumphant. Villains will continue to be thwarted, redskins will continue to bite the dust. And heroines will continue to smile coyly at heroes who clasp a six-shooter in one hand and a guitar in the other.

By way of proving all this, (and here, by the way, is the subject of this story) Republic's publicity chief, Mort Goodman, offered to take us to a location where a horse opera was in the throes of production.

Goodman was preoccupied with the prospects of having Orson Welles and other big stars of non-cowboy films on his lot, but he did take time as we drove to location to talk about westerns.

Cowboy stars have a caste system all their own. Today's top cowboy is Roy Rogers who, with his horse *Trigger*, is one of Hollywood's ten top boxoffice attractions. All Rogers' epics now are filmed in color, have large casts, and may cost the studio several hundred thousand dollars each. Rogers is the "King of the Cowboys," which struck us as a downright undemocratic appellation for a man who champions the underdog every time he draws a gun.

GENE AUTRY, another guitar and pony enthusiast, used to be the "king," but he joined the Army during the war and now that he's back in civilian boots has yet to attain his erstwhile popularity. Autry is leaving the Republic lot soon and will make his epics elsewhere. One lot apparently, isn't big enough for a king and an ex-king. Until his contract runs out, however, the Autry productions are in the higher cost brackets.

Republic once made a series of cowboy films starring one William Elliott as "Red Ryder." Elliott was so successful in these that he was graduated from the horse opera class. That is, his films now are in the million dollar class, and are called "westerns." Elliott, by the way, never cuddled a guitar in his horsey days.

Another "western," as differentiated from "horse opera" star, is John Wayne, an actor of high repute in Hollywood who makes Republic his home. Wayne has the right to produce his own pictures, and has taken advantage of that

right on occasion. He does, however, stick to western locales.

Back in the horse opera class, Republic has a couple of other cowboys who are rated as stars. One of these is Allen Lane, a non-guitar man. The other is Monte Hale, who can wield a guitar with the best of them. The studio thinks so much of Hale that all his films are done in color. This was the gentleman we were to watch emote.

WE DROVE into the Iverson Ranch, which offers a variety of western scenery—rocks, sand, hills, mountains, cliffs, rivers, lakes and other items nature destined for the pursuit of villains on horseback. At various times every studio in Hollywood has rented the Iverson ranch for the filming of westerns so that its rocks and streams are as familiar to horse opera lovers as their own living rooms. As we drove to a high plateau that had been marked out for the day's shooting, we passed abandoned buildings and corrals that had been used in movies. On some rocky hills, movie makers had added paper mache rocks to those already there in an effort to make nature look more natural. We half-expected to see an old guitar or discarded villain lying about, but were disappointed.

Finally we came upon the location company. There were several trucks, including one with a power generator and another with sound equipment, a crew of about 20 men to handle the equipment, several horses, several actors, the director, his assistant, a cameraman and his assistant, and several electricians, sound and otherwise.

A REHEARSAL was in progress on a strip of grass marked out as the set. A large canvas screen on a frame was directly over the camera. The screen made a square shadow on the ground where the actors stood. Electricians with lights illuminated the actors standing in the shadow to the proper intensity for the color film inside the camera.

We had arrived in time to watch the filming of a dramatic moment in the film, *Along the Oregon Trail.* The scene goes something like this:

Three Indians, one of whom is attired in a chief's headdress, three Indian

(Continued on Page 4)

It's romance when Roy Rogers serenades pretty Conchita Limus.

(Continued from Page 3)

ponies, the hero—our Monte—and villain Roy Barcroft are on stage. Barcroft hasn't shaved for ten days. He has a mean look in his eyes. Monte Hale is tall, a clean-cut American youth. He wears a buckskin shirt, homespun pants tucked into black boots, and spurs. The Indians are real Indians only more deadpanned. They wear buckskin shirts and pants and moccasins.

"Action," calls the director. Monte straightens his shoulders and grabs for a rifle in the villain's hands. They struggle for it. Injun chief snatches rifle from them.

Barcroft: Gimme it, it's mine.

Monte: He lies! He stole that rifle from Indian's brother.

Indian Chief: (holding palm of hand toward camera) Stop! (speaks in low monotone) Indian have way to find who tells truth. (pause to look at fellow Indians who are holding struggling Monte and villain apart.) Each man take rifle, mount ponies, ride 300 paces.

Barcroft: Yaa. What's the rest of it?

Indian Chief: Turn ponies and ride toward each other. Each man have one (holds up one finger) bullet in rifle.

Monte: (to Barcroft in "I dare you" manner) Are you scared? (pause) Takes rifle from Indian Chief, thrusts chin forward and glares at villain for full five seconds, turns sharply and strides out of camera range.

Barcroft: (returns Monte's stare villainously, crinkles eyes, grabs gun from another Indian and slouches out of camera range.)

AS THE rehearsal ended, Barcroft strode in our direction, laughing hysterically. "It's the dog-gondest thing!" he screamed, guffawing and slapping his thigh. "These things get funnier and funnier. I hardly can keep a straight face!"

The publicity man frowned at Barcroft, then introduced us. A mild-mannered fellow of about 40, Barcroft said he'd been in about 150 cowboy pictures as a villain, and had been killed or nearly killed in all of them. The director called for another rehearsal.

When they had finished, it was Monte himself who came in our direction. We were introduced.

"Haowdy," drawled Hale, a hearty fellow if there ever was one, "right happy to knaow yuh!" We shook hands.

"Haowdy," we said, in our best Chestnut street accent, and proceeded to ask how he got where he was.

Monte needed no urging. He was a strolling, guitar-playing singer in Texas when a War Bond show of Hollywood stars arrived in his "taown." They needed a git-tar player and hired one. One member of the company recommended him to Republic. He was hired. He played bits and parts in about twenty horse operas in the last three years and then he was starred in his own series of pictures. This *Along the Oregon Trail* is the first of a new series of eight pictures starring Monte. It was much longer the way he told it.

DURING the next rehearsal we paid special attention to the Indian Chief, whose name is Noble Johnson. He is the Indian who always is the Indian Chief in western pictures. The publicity man said Noble is 65 years old.

Finally they were ready to shoot. The director said mildly, "This is a take, boys. Roll 'em." Monte straightened his shoulders and his face assumed the wronged but honest look he was using for the scene. Roy Barcroft looked nasty as all get out. The sound truck bell clanged announcing the actors could start. Monte and Roy struggled, Johnson grabbed the gun, and just in the middle of his fantastic method of finding out which of them was lying, he forgot his lines. The "three hundred paces" threw him.

They did it again and the director said, "Print it." Indian Chief Noble Johnson stared out at the lovely hills on the Iverson Ranch, remarked to a fellow Indian: "Awful pretty out here, isn't it?"

MONTE was finishing the story of his life. A man dressed exactly as he was walked up and pointed at the belt Monte was wearing. Our hero stared for a moment questioning, then understood. "Oh," he said. "Double." He unhooked the belt and gave it to the man, who buckled it about his own waist.

The double mounted a horse. The director was ready to shoot the scene where the hero and villain rode 300 paces on horseback, then turned and rode toward each other, shooting their one bullet apiece.

As the double and Barcroft went through that scene we looked for Monte. He was playing poker with the electricians.

We have it on good authority, however, that he triumphs over the villain in the end.

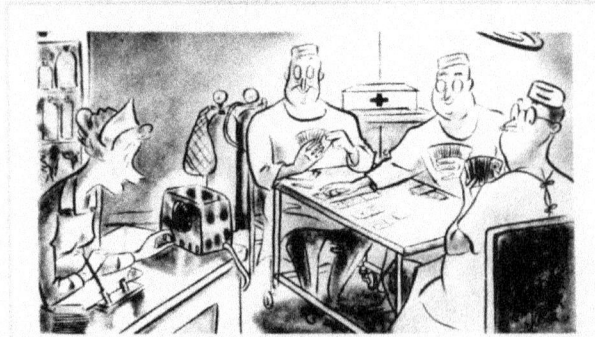

"Calling Dr. Alexander . . . Dr. Alexander . . . wanted in surgery . . ."

EVERYBODY'S WEEKLY, JULY 6, COPYRIGHT, 1947, THE PHILADELPHIA INQUIRER

The Philadelphia Inquirer, July 6, 1947

Will Hunt Rocks on Movie Ranch

San Fernando Valley Rocks and Gem Society wil meet Aug. 25 at the Iverson Movie Ranch off Santa Susana Pass near Chatsworth to hunt for sharks' teeth and fossil rocks.

Members will bring a picnic lunch and a tour will be made of the ranch. Each will also bring two rocks, one for the club's collection and the other to be given to underprivileged boys.

Left: The Valley News, August 19, 1956

Right: The Algona Upper Des Moines, September 27, 1951

Just came in from Iverson's Ranch, near Chatsworth, Cal., where we visited "The Lone Star Lawman" set. Arriving at lunch time, we watched the line form at the portable steam-table.

Anyone not familiar with moving picture company procedure would wonder why Producer Vincent M. Fennelly, Director Lewis Collins and Stars Johnny Mack Brown and Jimmy Ellison were on the tail end of the line.

Laborers, grips, prop-men and working crew always eat first. There's a very good reason. Lunch period for these workers consists of only a half-hour. Then, they hurry back to line up the technical equipment in preparation for the first shot after lunch. Gains a half-hour of sunlight!

Stars, producer and director have a full hour and can finish eating while the boys are getting "set-up" for them. Oddly enough, Melvin Shyer, first assistant director, is last man to eat. Although he's first to return to the set, he must see that everyone is fed. Drivers, en-route from studio, and set-watchmen must have lunches saved out before "seconds" are served. Open-air shooting breeds healthy appetites. Says Shyer, "If we ran short, I'd have mutiny on my hands!"

* * *

GEORGE MAHARIS, co-star of "Route 66" clowns in shallow lake during filming. Comedian Buster Keaton (nearly submerged) is shown with a grin—something that he is never shown doing on the screen. The latter will be one of the guest stars in a "Route 66" series show.

'Route 66' Aims For Laughs

HOLLYWOOD — The Friday night "Route 66" series has never been known for laughs or even small titters, but this fall the show broke precedent with "Journey to Nineveh," starring, sad, stone-faced Buster Keaton, big mouth Joe E. Brown and pudgy Edgar Buchanan.

The plot isn't involved and starts out with heroes Buz Murdock and Tod Stiles driving down a highway minding their own business when they see a hitchhiker. Keaton, and decide to give him a lift.

Keaton is one jinxed character. The boys almost immediately have a flat tire. While jacking up the car, the wheel falls off and goes hurtling down the road. One obstruction builds upon another in the true manner of the old silent comedies. Whatever Keaton does disaster follows.

One sunny day this summer the 66 crew filmed a fishing sequence Keaton had dreamed up for the show. This took place at Iverson's Ranch 30 miles from Hollywood on a small lake with a black silt bottom six feet under water at its deepest point.

Buster, wearing his traditional costume of a small pork pie hat with a black band, a black vest ripped in the rear, hopped into a tiny dinghy while George Mahar-

is, holding a fishing line, tried not to laugh out loud.

Then Keaton crouched over the oars and explained how he would swamp the boat out in the lake. The cameras moved in and Buster slid the dinghy down the grass into the water.

The idea for this silent sequence was to have Keaton snarl his fishing line, and in his efforts to untangle the mess, he would swamp the boat. For the most part Maharis would merely be an onlooker and an obstacle in the tiny boat.

Once out in the water Keaton went to work with dazzling efficiency as he squirmed about trying to unloosen the snarled line. Within a minute the boat was half under water, and soon the men were touching the bottom. Keaton's intensive, sour face never moved a muscle when the camera finished up with a shot of the exasperated man, surrounded by floating oars and a few inches of a swamped dinghy.

Then, breaking tradition, Maharis, soaking wet, holding the fishing line, and Keaton, squatting on his knees in the water, broke into grins. However, this shot did not appear in the show. Keaton can never laugh on the screen.

If Keaton fans are patient they soon may be seeing some of the comics' old two-reelers and big silent movies like "The General," and "The Navigator," a masterpiece. Buster is planning to show them first abroad. "Five London theaters are scheduled to show 'The General' at once," says Buster. "If I get a good reception, we'll show 'em here. The films are in fine shape and the prints are excellent."

The old prat-fall and the big laughs may be coming back. At least "66" is giving it a try.

Above: The Manhattan Mercury, October 5, 1962

Right: The Des Moines Register, September 23, 1944

IN HOLLYWOOD
'Strip Tease' By Martha

By Ernest Foster.

HOLLYWOOD, CAL. (U.P.)— Wearing yards of billowy pink organdie over a bustle, voluminous petticoats and a whalebone corset that pinched her waistline to a slim 23 inches, Martha O'Driscoll looked like a luscious strawberry ice cream cone.

The setting is Iverson Ranch, 40 miles from Hollywood, where Universal is making "musical Roundup."

MARTHA O'DRISCOLL.

The ranch is an expanse of western country consisting mainly of rocks, sagebrush and heat. It's as authentic a duplicate of Arizona range in the year 1870 as you can find today, without going to Arizona.

Miss O'Driscoll was wearing her fancy outfit to church when a couple of Leo Carrillo's outlaws kidnaped her.

But as Martha stepped gingerly on a flat-topped rock, the horse looked suspicious.

She lifted a shapely foot to the stirrup and hoisted herself up, side saddle. She gave the reluctant mount a few kicks in the flank, and he was off.

"He was too slow in starting," decided Director Jean Yarbrough. "Let's try it again."

In dismounting the ruffle at the neck of Martha's dress caught on the saddle horn and TORE WITH A HEART-RENDING SOUND. There was a general moan from the company.

"Edna," yelled the director.

Edna, the wardrobe attendant, came a-running with a safety pin and fastened the ruffle. Mending it would delay production.

The scene was repeated several times, and each time a little more of Martha's frock came apart.

All this time Noah Berry, Jr., Martha's boy friend in the film, was watching the proceedings from a fence rail.

"Hell," he drawled to the director when the scene was finished "how do you expect anyone to see me in this picture with Gypsy Rose O'Driscoll doing a striptease?"

Above: **Tarzan's Secret Treasure** (1941)
Below: **Perils of Nyoka** (1942)

Above: **Adventures of Captain Marvel** (1941)
Below: **Stagecoach** (1939)

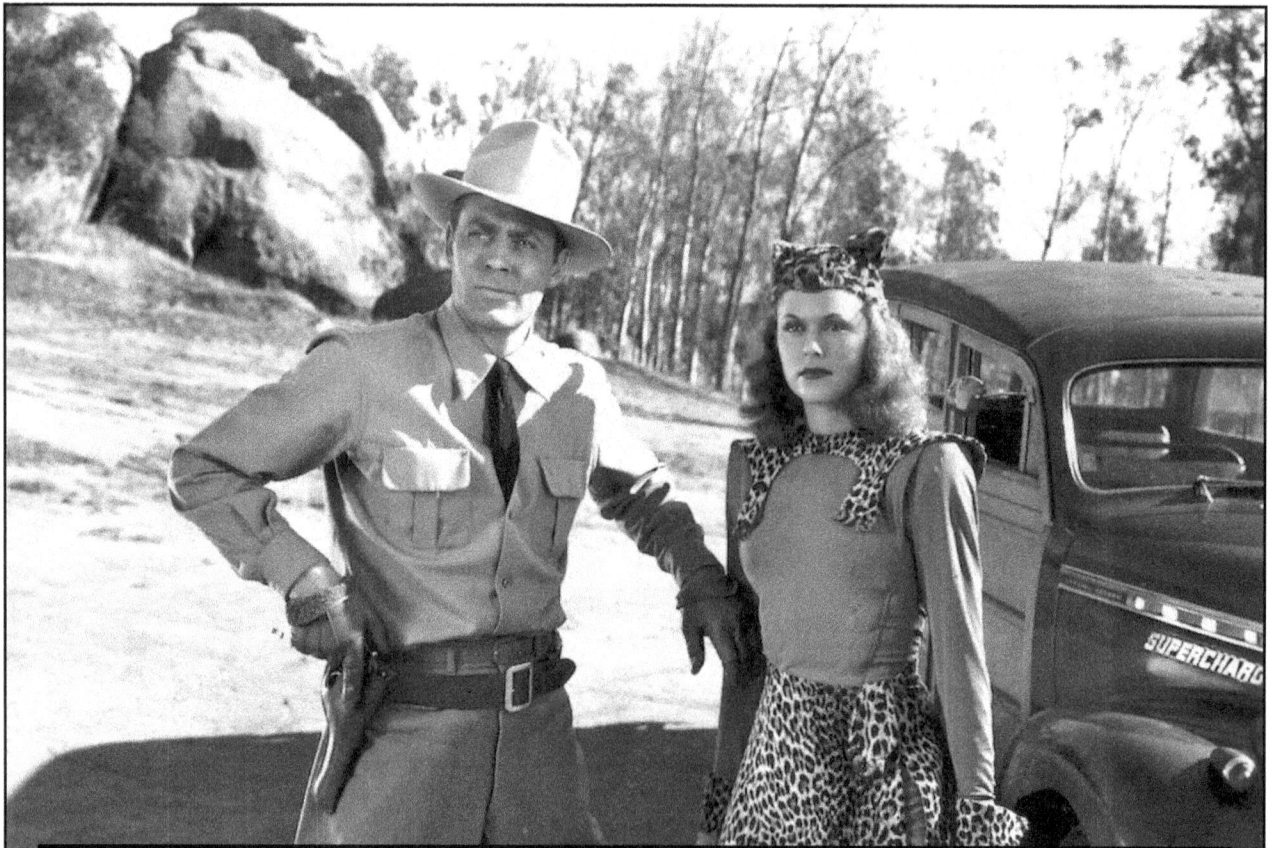

Above: **The Tiger Woman** (1944)
Below: **Man In the Saddle** (1951)

FILMOGRAPHY

ALPHABETICAL LISTING

* Denotes a possible Iverson Ranch sighting in the film

20 Million Miles to Earth (Columbia 1957) William Hopper
30 Foot Bride of Candy Rock, The (Columbia 1959) Lou Costello
A Double-Dyed Deceiver (Goldwyn 1920) Jack Pickford
A Thousand and One Nights (Columbia 1945) Cornel Wilde
Abbott and Costello Meet the Keystone Kops (Universal 1955) Abbott & Costello
Abilene Trail (Monogram 1951) Whip Wilson
Across the Badlands (Columbia 1950) Charles Starrett
Across The Sierras (Columbia 1941) William Elliott
Adventures in Silverado (Columbia 1948) William Bishop
Adventures of Captain Africa (Columbia 1955) John Hart
Adventures of Captain Marvel (Republic 1941) Tom Tyler
Adventures of Frank and Jesse James (Republic 1948) Clayton Moore
Adventures of Red Ryder (Republic 1940) Don Red Barry
Adventures of Spin and Marty, The (Disney 1955) Tim Considine
Adventures of the Masked Phantom, The (Equity 1939) Monte Rawlins
African Treasure (Monogram 1952) John Sheffield
Al Jennings of Oklahoma (Columbia 1951) Dan Duryea
Albuquerque (Paramount 1948) Randolph Scott
Ali Baba Goes to Town (20th Century-Fox 1937) Eddie Cantor
Alias Billy the Kid (Republic 1946) Sunset Carson
Alias Jesse James (United Artists 1959) Bob Hope
Along Came Jones (United Artists 1945) Gary Cooper
Along the Oregon Trail (Republic 1947) Monte Hale
Along the Sundown Trail (PRC 1942) Art Davis
Ambush (MGM 1949) Robert Taylor
Ambush at Cimarron Pass (20th Century-Fox 1958) Scott Brady
Annie Oakley (RKO 1935) Barbara Stanwyck
Apache Ambush (Columbia 1955) Bill Williams
Apache Kid, The (Republic 1941) Donald Barry
Apache Rose (Republic 1947) Roy Rogers
Apache War Smoke (MGM 1952) Gilbert Roland
Apache Woman, The (American Releasing Corp 1955) Joan Taylor
Arizona Cowboy, The (Republic 1950) Rex Allen
Arizona Cyclone (Universal 1941) Dick Curtis
Arizona Kid, The (20th Century-Fox 1930) Carol Lombard
Arizona Kid, The (Republic 1939) Roy Rogers
Arizona Legion (RKO 1939) George O'Brien
Arizona Manhunt (Republic 1951) Michael Chapin

Arizona Stagecoach (Monogram 1942) Ray Corrigan
Arizona Territory (Monogram 1950) Whip Wilson
Arizona Terrors (Republic 1942) Donald Barry
Arizonian, The (RKO 1935) Richard Dix
Army Girl (Republic 1938) Madge Evans
Arrow in the Dust (Allied Artists 1954) Sterling Hayden
Atom Man vs Superman (Columbia 1950) Kirk Alyn
Avenging Rider, The (RKO 1943) Tim Holt
Avenging Waters (Columbia 1936) Ken Maynard
Back in the Saddle (Republic 1941) Gene Autry
Bad Man of Deadwood (Republic 1941) Roy Rogers
Bad Men of Missouri (Warner Bros 1941) Dennis Morgan
Bad Men of the Border (Universal 1945) Kirby Grant
Bad Men of the Hills (Columbia 1942) Russell Hayden
Bad Men of Tombstone (Allied Artists 1949) Barry Sullivan
Badman's Country (Warner Bros 1958) George Montgomery
Balloonatic, The (Metro 1923) Buster Keaton
Bandit King of Texas (Republic 1949) Alan Rocky Lane
Bandit Trail, The (RKO 1941) Tim Holt
Bandits of Dark Canyon (Republic 1947) Allan Lane
Bandits of El Dorado (Columbia 1949) Charles Starrett
Bandits of the Badlands (Republic 1945) Sunset Carson
Bandits of the West (Republic 1953) Allan Lane
Bar 20 Rides Again (Paramount 1935) William Boyd
Bar Z Bad Men (Republic 1937) Johnny Mack Brown
Batman (Columbia 1943) Lewis Wilson
Batman and Robin (Columbia 1949) Robert Lowery
Battle of Rogue River (Columbia 1954) George Montgomery
Battle of the Coral Sea (Columbia 1959) Cliff Robertson
Beauty and the Bandit (Monogram 1946) Gilbert Roland
Behold My Wife! (Paramount 1934) Sylvia Sidney
Belle Starr (20th Century Fox 1941) Randolph Scott
Belle Starr's Daughter (20th Century-Fox 1947) George Montgomery
Bells of Rosarita, The (Republic 1945) Roy Rogers
Ben Hur: A Tale of the Christ (MGM 1925) Ramon Navarro
Beneath Western Skies (Republic 1944) Robert Livingston
Bengal Brigade (Universal 1954) Rock Hudson
Beyond the Last Frontier (Republic 1943) Eddie Dew
Beyond the Sacramento (Columbia 1940) William Elliott
Big Bonanza, The (Republic 1944) Richard Arlen
Big Noise, The (20th Century Fox 1944) Laurel & Hardy
Big Show, The (Republic 1936) Gene Autry

Big Steal, The (RKO 1950) Robert Mitchum
Billy the Kid in Texas (PRC 1940) Bob Steele
Billy the Kid Outlawed (PRC 1940) Bob Steele
Billy the Kid Returns (Republic 1938) Roy Rogers
Billy the Kid Trapped (PRC 1942) Buster Crabbe
Billy the Kid Wanted (PRC 1941) Bob Steele
Billy the Kid's Fighting Pals (PRC 1941) Bob Steele
Billy the Kid's Gun Justice (PRC 1940) Bob Steele
Billy the Kid's Range War (PRC 1941) Bob Steele
Bitter Creek (Allied Artists 1954) William Elliott
Black Arrow (Columbia 1944) Mark Roberts
Black Bandit, The (Universal 1938) Bob Baker
Black Bart (Universal 1948) Yvonne de Carlo
Black Dakotas, The (Columbia 1954) Gary Merrill
Black Eagle (Columbia 1948) William Bishop
Black Hills (Eagle Lion 1947) Eddie Dean
Black Hills Ambush (Republic 1952) Allan Lane
Black Hills Express (Republic 1943) Donald Barry
Black Lash, The (Western Adventure 1951) Lash LaRue
Black Parachute, The (Columbia 1944) John Carradine
Black Spurs (Paramount 1965) Rory Calhoun
Black Watch, The (Fox 1929) Victor McLaglen
Black Whip, The (Regal 1956) Paul Richards
Black Widow, The (Republic 1947) Bruce Edwards
Blackhawk (Columbia 1952) Kirk Alyn
Blackjack Ketchum, Desperado (Columbia 1956) Howard Duff
Blazing Across the Pecos (Columbia 1948) Charles Starrett
Blazing Bullets (Monogram 1951) Johnny Mack Brown
Blazing Guns (Kent 1935) Reb Russell
Blazing Six Shooters (Columbia 1940) Charles Starrett
Blazing Sixes (Warner Bros 1937) Dick Foran
Blazing the Overland Trail (Columbia 1956) Lee Roberts
Blazing Trail, The (Columbia 1949) Charles Starrett
Blocked Trail, The (Republic 1943) Bob Steele
Blood Arrow (20th Century-Fox 1958) Scott Brady
Blood on the Moon (RKO 1948) Robert Mitchum
Bold Caballero, The (Republic 1936) Robert Livingston
Bold Frontiersman, The (Republic 1948) Allan Lane
Bomba and the Jungle Girl (Monogram 1952) John Sheffield
Bonanza Town (Columbia 1951) Charles Starrett
Boots Malone (Columbia 1952) William Holden
Border Feud (PRC 1947) Lash LaRue

Border Legion, The (Republic 1940) Roy Rogers
Border Rangers (Lippert 1950) Donald Barry
Border Saddlemates (Republic 1952) Rex Allen
Bordertown Gun Fighters (Republic 1943) William Elliott
Bordertown Trail (Republic 1944) Sunset Carson
Boss of Boomtown (Universal 1944) Rod Cameron
Boss of Bullion City (Universal 1941) Johnny Mack Brown
Bounty Hunter, The (Warner Bros 1954) Randolph Scott
Branded (Columbia 1931) Buck Jones
Brass Legend, The (United Artists 1956) Hugh O'Brien
Bride Wore Red, The (MGM 1937) Joan Crawford
Broken Arrow (20th Century-Fox 1950) James Stewart
Broken Lance (20th Century-Fox 1954) Spencer Tracy
Buckaroo Sheriff of Texas (Republic 1951) Michael Chapin
Buckskin Lady, The (United Artists 1957) Patricia Medina
Buffalo Bill in Tomahawk Territory (United Artists 1952) Clayton Moore
Buffalo Bill Rides Again (Screen Guild 1947) Richard Arlen
Bullet Code (RKO 1940) George O'Brien
Bullets and Saddles (Monogram 1943) Ray Corrigan
Bullets for Bandits (Columbia 1942) William Elliott
Bullets for Rustlers (Columbia 1940) Charles Starrett
Bury Me Not on the Lone Prairie (Universal 1941) Johnny Mack Brown
Calamity Jane and Sam Bass (Universal 1949) Yvonne De Carlo
Calamity Jane and the Texan (Columbia 1950) Evelyn Ankers
California (Paramount 1946) Ray Milland
California Firebrand (Republic 1948) Monte Hale
California Gold Rush (Republic 1946) William Elliott
California Joe (Republic 1943) Donald Barry
California Mail, The (Warner Bros 1936) Dick Foran
California Passage (Republic 1950) Forrest Tucker
California Trail, The (Columbia 1933) Buck Jones
Californian, The (20th Century-Fox 1937) Ricardo Cortez
Call of the Rockies (Columbia 1938) Charles Starrett
Call of the Rockies (Republic 1944) Sunset Carson
Call the Mesquiteers (Republic 1938) Three Mesquiteers
Callaway Went Thataway (MGM 1951) Fred MacMurray
Calling All Marines (Republic 1939) Donald Barry
Calling Wild Bill Elliott (Republic 1943) William Elliott
Canyon Ambush (Monogram 1952) Johnny Mack Brown
Canyon City (Republic 1943) Donald Barry
Canyon Raiders (Allied Artists 1956) Whip Wilson
Captain American (Republic 1943) Dick Purcell

Captain Fury (United Artists 1939) Brian Aherne
Captain Midnight (Columbia 1942) Dave O'Brien
Captain Video, Master of the Stratosphere (Columbia 1952) Judd Holdren
Captive of Billy the Kid (Republic 1952) Allan Lane
Caravan Trail, The (PRC 1946) Eddie Dean
Carson City (Warner Bros 1953) Randolph Scott
Carson City Cyclone (Republic 1943) Donald Barry
Carson City Kid (Republic 1940) Roy Rogers
Carson City Raiders (Republic 1948) Allan Lane
Cast a Long Shadow (United Artists 1959) Audie Murphy
Cattle Queen (United Artists 1951) Maria Hart
Cattle Queen of Montana (RKO 1954) Barbara Stanwyck
Cavalcade of the West (Grand National 1936) Hoot Gibson
Cave of Outlaws (Universal 1951) Macdonald Carey
Challenge of the Range (Colubmia 1949) Charles Starrett
Charge of the Light Brigade, The (Warner Bros 1936) Errol Flynn
Chatterbox (Republic 1943) Joe E. Brown
Check Your Guns (PRC 1947) Eddie Dean
Cherokee Flash, The (Republic 1937) Sunset Carson
Cherokee Strip (Paramount 1940) Richard Dix
Cherokee Strip, The (Warner Bros 1937) Dick Foran
Cherokee Uprising (Monogram 1950) Whip Wilson
Chetniks! The Fighting Guerillas (20th Century Fox 1943) Philip Dorn
Cheyenne Kid, The (Monogram 1940) Jack Randall
Cheyenne Kid, The (Radio 1933) Tom Keene
Cheyenne Rides Again (Victory 1937) Tom Tyler
Cheyenne Roundup (Universal 1943) Johnny Mack Brown
Cheyenne Takes Over (Eagle-Lion 1947) Lash LaRue
Cheyenne Wildcat (Republic 1944) William Elliott
Chicago Kid, The (Republic 1945) Donald Barry
China (Paramount 1943) Loretta Young
China's Little Devils (Monogram 1945) Harry Carey
Chip of the Flying U (Universal 1939) Johnny Mack Brown
Cisco Kid, The (Fox 1931) Warner Baxter
Clash of the Wolves (Warner Bros 1925) Rin Tin Tin
Code of the Fearless (Spectrum 1939) Tom Tyler
Code of the Lawless (Universal 1945) Kirby Grant
Code of the Outlaw (Republic 1942) Bob Steele
Code of the Prairie (Republic 1944) Sunset Carson
Code of the Secret Service (Warner Bros 1939) Ronald Reagan
Code of the Silver Sage (Republic 1950) Allan Lane
Cole Younger, Gunfighter (Allied Artists 1958) Frank Lovejoy

Colorado Ambush (Monogram 1951) Johnny Mack Brown
Colorado Pioneers (Republic 1945) William Elliott
Colorado Ranger (Lippert 1950) Jimmy Ellison
Colt 45 (Warner Bros 1950) Randolph Scott
Come On, Cowboys (Republic 1937) Three Mesquiteers
Come On, Danger (Radio Pictures 1932) Tom Keene
Come On, Danger! (RKO 1942) Tim Holt
Come On, Leathernecks! (Republic 1938) Richard Cromwell
Come On, Rangers (Republic 1938) Roy Rogers
Congo Bill (Columbia 1948) Don McGuire
Conquest of Cheyenne (Republic 1946) William Elliott
Cornered (Columbia 1932) Tim McCoy
Coroner Creek (Columbia 1948) Randolph Scott
Corpus Christi Bandits (Republic 1945) Allan Lane
Country Beyond, The (20th Century-Fox 1936) Rochelle Hudson
Covered Wagon Days (Republic 1940) Robert Livingston
Covered Wagon Raid (Republic 1950) Allan Lane
Covered Wagon, The (Paramount 1923) J. Warren Kerrigan
Cow Country (Allied Artists 1953) Edmond O'Brien
Cow Town (Columbia 1950) Gene Autry
Cowboy and the Lady, The (United Artists 1938) Gary Cooper
Cowboy and the Prizefighter (Eagle Lion 1949) Jim Bannon
Cowboy and the Senorita (Republic 1944) Roy Rogers
Cowboy in the Clouds (Columbia 1943) Charles Starrett
Cowboy Serenade (Republic 1942) Gene Autry
Cowboy Star, The (Columbia 1936) Charles Starrett
Cowboys from Texas (Republic 1939) Robert Livingston
Crashing Thru (Monogram 1949) Whip Wilson
Crashout (Hal E Chester Productions 1955) William Bendix
Crimson Ghost, The (Republic 1946) Charles Quigley
Cripple Creek (Columbia 1952) William Bishop
Crooked River (Lippert 1950) Jimmy Ellison
Custer's Last Stand (Weiss Productions 1936) Rex Lease
Cyclone Fury (Columbia 1951) Charles Starrett
Cyclone Kid, The (Republic 1942) Donald Barry
Cyclone Ranger, The (Spectrum 1935) Bill Cody
Dakota (Republic 1945) John Wayne
Dakota Kid, The (Republic 1951) Michael Chapin
Dallas (Warner Bros 1950) Gary Cooper
Dalton Gang, The (Lippert 1949) Donald Barry
Daltons Ride Again, The (Universal 1945) Alan Curtis
Daltons' Women, The (Western Adventures 1950) Lash LaRue

Daniel Boone (RKO 1936) George O'Brien
Daredevils of the West (Republic 1943) Allan Lane
Daring Dobermans, The (Rosamond Productions 1973) Charles Knox Robinson
Darkest Africa (Republic 1936) Clyde Beatty
Daughter of Don Q (Republic 1946) Kirk Alyn
Davy Crockett, Indian Scout (United Artists 1950) George Montgomery
Dawn Rider, The (Monogram 1935) John Wayne
Days of Buffalo Bill (Republic 1946) Sunset Carson
Days of Jesse James (Republic 1939) Roy Rogers
Days of Old Cheyenne (Republic 1943) Donald Barry
Dead Man's Gold (Screen Guild 1947) Lash LaRue
Dead Man's Gulch (Republic 1943) Donald Barry
Dead Man's Trail (Monogram 1952) Johnny Mack Brown
Deadwood Dick (Columbia 1940) Don Douglas
Death Rides the Plains (PRC 1943) Robert Livingston
Death Valley Gunfighter (Republic 1949) Allan Lane
Death Valley Manhunt (Republic 1943) William Eliott
Death Valley Outlaws (Republic 1941) Donald Barry
Deathsport (New World Pictures 1978) David Carradine
Denver Kid, The (Republic 1948) Rocky Lane
Deputy Marshal (Lippert 1949) Jon Hall
Desert Bandit (Republic 1941) Donald Barry
Desert Gold (Paramount 1936) Buster Crabbe
Desert Horseman, The (Columbia 1946) Charles Starrett
Desert Love (Fox 1920) Tom Mix
Desert of Lost Men (Republic 1951) Allan Lane
Desert Passage (RKO 1952) Tim Holt
Desert Vigilante (Columbia 1949) Charles Starrett
Desire (Paramount 1936) Gary Cooper
Desperado, The (Allied Artists 1954) Wayne Morris
Desperadoes of Dodge City (Republic 1948) Allan Lane
Desperadoes of the West (Republic 1950) Richard Powers
Desperadoes' Outpost (Republic 1952) Allan Lane
Devil Horse, The (Hal Roach 1926) Rex the Wonder Horse
Devil Horse, The (Mascot 1932) Harry Carey
Devil Riders (PRC 1943) Buster Crabbe
Devil's Trail, The (Columbia 1942) William Elliott
Dick Tracy vs Crime Inc (Republic 1941) Ralph Byrd
Do and Dare (Fox 1922) Tom Mix
Domino Kid, The (Columbia 1957) Rory Calhoun
Don Daredevil Rides Again (Republic 1951) Ken Curtis
Don't Knock the Rock (Clover Productions 1956) Bill Halen and the Comets

Doolins of Oklahoma, The (Columbia 1949) Randolph Scott
Doomed at Sundown (Republic 1937) Bob Steele
Down Laredo Way (Republic 1953) Rex Allen
Down Rio Grande Way (Columbia 1942) Charles Starrett
Dragonfly Squadron (Allied Artists 1954) John Hodiak
Drifter, The (PRC 1944) Buster Crabbe
Driftin' River (PRC 1946) Eddie Dean
Drifting Along (Monogram 1946) Johnny Mack Brown
Drum Beat (Warner Bros 1954) Alan Ladd
Drums Across the River (Universal 1954) Audie Murphy
Drums of Fu Manchu (Republic 1940) Henry Brandon
Drums of the Desert (Monogram 1940) Ralph Byrd
Dude Goes West (Allied Artists 1948) Eddie Albert
Dude Ranger, The (Fox 1934) George O'Brien
Dudes Are Pretty People (United Artists 1942) Jimmy Rogers
Duel at Apache Wells (Republic 1957) Anna Maria Alberghetti
Duel at Silver Creek (Universal 1952) Audie Murphy
Durango Valley Raiders (Republic 1938) Bob Steele
El Paso (Paramount 1949) John Payne
El Paso Kid, The (Republic 1946) Sunset Carson
El Paso Stampede (Republic 1953) Allan Lane
Elfego Baca: Six Gun Law (Buena Vista 1962) Robert Loggia
Elmo, the Mighty (Universal 1919) Elmo Lincoln
Empty Holsters (Warner Bros 1937) Dick Foran
Escape from Red Rock (20th Century-Fox 1958) Brian Donlevy
Escort West (United Artists 1959) Victor Mature
Everybody's Dancin' (Lippert 1950) Donald Barry
Fabulous Texan, The (Republic 1947) William Elliott
Far Frontier, The (Republic 1948) Roy Rogers
Fargo (Monogram 1952) William Elliott
Fargo Express (Fox 1933) Ken Maynard
Fargo Kid, The (RKO 1940) Tim Holt
Fast Bullets (Reliable 1936) Tom Tyler
Fast on the Draw (Lippert 1950) Jimmy Shamrock Ellison
Feathered Serpent, The (Monogram 1949) Roland Winters
Federal Agents vs Underworld Inc (Republic 1949) Kirk Alyn
Fence Riders (Monogram 1950) Whip Wilson
Feud Maker, The (Republic 1938) Bob Steele
Fighting Bill Fargo (Universal 1942) Johnny Mack Brown
Fighting Buckaroo, The (Columbia 1943) Charles Starrett
Fighting Frontier (RKO 1943) Tim Holt
Fighting Frontiersman, The (Columbia 1946) Charles Starrett

Fighting Gringo, The (RKO 1938) George O'Brien
Fighting Man of the Plains (20th Century-Fox 1949) Randolph Scott
Fighting Redhead, The (Eagle Lion 1949) Jim Bannon
Fighting Seabees, The (Republic 1944) John Wayne
Fighting Sheriff, The (Columbia 1931) Buck Jones
Fighting Texan, The (Ambassador 1937) Kermit Maynard
Fighting Through (Kent 1934) Reb Russell
Fighting Vigilantes, The (Eagle Lion 1947) Lash LaRue
Fighting With Kit Carson (Mastoc 1933) Johnny Mack Brown
Firebrands of Arizona (Republic 1944) Sunset Carson
Firefly, The (MGM 1937) Jeanette MacDonald
Five Guns to Tombstone (United Artists 1960) James Brown
Five Guns West (American International 1955) John Lund
Flaming Feather (Paramount 1951) Sterling Hayden
Flaming Guns (Universal 1932) Tom Mix
Flashing Guns (Monogram 1947) Johnny Mack Brown
Flesh and the Spur (American International 1956) John Agar
Flight Into Nowhere (Columbia 1938) Jack Holt
Flying Disc Man From Mars (Republic 1950) Walter Reed
Flying Dueces (RKO 1939) Laurel and Hardy
Flying Elephants (Roach 1928) Laurel and Hardy
Flying Serpent, The (PRC 1946) George Zucco
Follow Me, Boys! (Buena Vista 1966) Fred MacMurray
Fort Dodge Stampede (Republic 1951) Allan Lane
Fort Vengeance (Allied Artists 1953) Keith Larsen
Fort Worth (Warner Bros 1951) Randolph Scott
Forty-Niners, The (Allied Artists 1954) William Elliott
Four Guns to the Border (Universal 1954) Rory Calhoun
Fourth Horseman, The (Universal 1932) Tom Mix
Freighters of Destiny (RKO Pathe 1931) Tom Keene
Frisco Tornado (Republic 1950) Allan Lane
From Hell to Texas (20th Century Fox 1958) Don Murray
Frontier Crusader (PRC 1940) Tim McCoy
Frontier Fugitives (PRC 1945) Texas Rangers
Frontier Investigator (Republic 1949) Allan Lane
Frontier Phantom, The (Western Adventure 1952) Lash LaRue
Frontier Pony Express (Republic 1939) Roy Rogers
Frontier Revenge (Screen Guild 1947) Lash La Rue
Frontier Vengeance (Republic 1940) Donald Barry
Frontiers of '49 (Columbia 1939) William Elliott
Fugitive from Sonora (Republic 1943) Donald Barry
Fugitive Sheriff, The (Columbia 1936) Ken Maynard

Fugitive Valley (Monogram 1941) Range Busters
Fury at Showdown (United Artists 1957) John Derek
Gallant Legion, The (Republic 1948) William Eliott
Gambler Wore a Gun, The (United Artists 1961) Jim Davis
Gambling Terror, The (Republic 1937) Johnny Mack Brown
Gangs of Sonora (Republic 1941) Robert Livingston
Garden of Allah, The (Selznick 1936) Marlene Dietrich
Gaucho, The (United Artists 1927) Mary Pickford
Gauchos of El Dorado (Republic 1941) Bob Steele
Gay Amigo, The (United Artists 1949) Duncan Reynaldo
Gay Cavalier, The (Monogram 1946) Gilbert Roland
Geronimo (Paramount 1940) Preston Foster
Ghost Guns (Monogram 1944) Johnny Mack Brown
Ghost of Zorro (Republic 1949) Clayton Moore
Ghost Town (United Artists 1956) Kent Taylor
Ghost Town Gold (Republic 1936) Three Mesquiteers
Ghost Town Renegades (PRC 1947) Lash LaRue
Ghost Town Riders (Universal 1938) Bob Baker
Ghost Valley Raiders (Republic 1940) Donald Barry
Gilded Lily, The (Paramount 1935) Claudette Colbert
Girl From Havana (Republic 1940) Dennis O'Keefe
Git Along Little Doggies (Republic 1937) Gene Autry
Glory Trail, The (Crescent 1936) Tom Keene
G-Men Never Forget (Republic 1948) Clayton Moore
Go West, Young Lady (Columbia 1941) Glenn Ford
Gold Raiders (Columbia 1951) Three Stooges
Golden Stallion, The (Republic 1949) Roy Rogers
Government Agents vs Phantom Legion (Republic 1951) Walter Reed
Grand Canyon Trail (Republic 1948) Roy Rogers
Grandpa Goes to Town (Republic 1940) James Gleason
Grapes of Wrath, The (20th Century-Fox 1940) Henry Fonda
Great Adventures of Captain Kidd, The (Columbia 1953) Richard Crane
Great Adventures of Wild Bill Hickok, The (Columbia 1938) William Elliott
Great Alaskan Mystery, The (Universal 1944) Milburn Stone
Great Stagecoach Robbery, The (Republic 1945) William Elliott
Great Train Robbery, The (Republic 1941) Bob Steele
Green Goddess, The (Warner Bros 1930) George Arliss
Gun Belt (United Artists 1953) George Montgomery
Gun Code (PRC 1940) Tim McCoy
Gun Duel in Durango (United Artists 1957) George Montgomery
Gun Fever (United Artists 1958) Mark Stevens
Gun Law (Majestic 1933) Jack Hoxie

Gun Smoke (Monogram 1945) Johnny Mack Brown
Gun Talk (Monogram 1947) Johnny Mack Brown
Gun That Won the West, The (Columbia 1955)
Gun Town (Universal 1946) Kirby Grant
Gunfight at Comanche Creek (Allied Artists 1963) Audie Murphy
Gunfighters of Abilene (United Artists 1959) Buster Crabbe
Gunfire (Lippert 1950) Donald Barry
Gunfire (Resolute 1935) Rex Bell
Gunman, The (Monogram 1952) Whip Wilson
Gunman's Code (Universal 1946) Kirby Grant
Gunmen from Laredo (Columbia 1959) Robert Knapp
Gunmen of Abilene (Republic 1950) Allan Lane
Gunning for Vengeance (Columbia 1946) Charles Starrett
Gunplay (RKO 1951) Tim Holt
Guns in the Dark (Republic 1937) Johnny Mack Brown
Guns of Fort Petticoat, The (Columbia 1957) Audie Murphy
Guns of the Pecos (Warner Bros 1937) Dick Foran
Gunslingers (Monogram 1950) Whip Wilson
Gunsmoke in Tucson (Allied Artists 1958) Mark Stevens
Gunsmoke Ranch (Republic 1937) Three Mesquiteers
Gunsmoke Trail (Monogram 1938) Jack Randall
Hail to the Rangers (Columbia 1943) Charles Starrett
Hands Across the Border (Republic 1944) Roy Rogers
Hands Across the Rockies (Columbia 1941) William Elliott
Hangman's Knot (Columbia 1952) Randolph Scott
Hannah Lee (Realart 1953) John Ireland
Harum Scarum (MGM 1965) Elvis Presley
Harvey Girls, The (MGM 1946) Judy Garland
Haunted Harbor (Republic 1940) Kane Richmond
Haunted Trails (Monogram 1949) Whip Wilson
Have Rocket Will Travel (Columbia 1959) Three Stooges
Hawk of Powder River, The (Eagle Lion 1948) Eddie Dean
Hawk of the Wilderness (Republic 1938) Herman Brix
Hawk of Wild River, The (Columbia 1952) Charles Starrett
Heading West (Columbia 1946) Charles Starrett
Heart of the Rio Grande (Republic 1942) Gene Autry
Heart of the Rockies (Republic 1937) Three Mesquiteers
Heir to Trouble (Columbia 1935) Ken Maynard
Heldorado (Republic 1946) Roy Rogers
Heldorado (Republic 1946) Roy Rogers
Hell's Crossroads (Republic 1957) Stephen McNally
Hell's Outpost (Republic 1954) Rod Cameron

Hellfire (Republic 1949) William Elliott
Henry Goes Arizona (MGM 1939) Frank Morgan
Heroes of the Saddle (Republic 1940) Robert Livingston
Hidden City, The (Monogram 1950) John Sheffield
Hidden Valley Outlaws (Republic 1944) William Elliott
High Noon (United Artists 1952) Gary Cooper
High, Wide and Handsome (Paramount 1937) Irene Dunne
Hills of Utah, The (Columbia 1951) Gene Autry
Hit the Saddle (Republic 1937) Three Mesquiteers
Hi-Yo Silver (Republic 1937) Lee Powell
Holt of the Secret Service (Columbia 1941) Jack Holt
Home in San Antone (Columbia 1949) Roy Acuff
Home on the Range (Republic 1946) Monte Hale
Homecoming (MGM 1948) Clark Gable
Homesteaders of Paradise Valley (Republic 1947) Allan Lane
Homesteaders, The (Allied Artists 1953) William Elliott
Horsemen of the Sierras (Columbia 1949) Charles Starrett
Hostile Country (Lippert 1950) Jimmy Ellison
Hot Lead (RKO 1951) Tim Holt
Hurricane Horseman (Kent 1931) Lane Chandler
I Killed Wild Bill Hickock (Associated Artists 1956) John Forbes
I Shot Billy the Kid (Lippert 1950) Donald Barry
I Shot Jesse James (Lippert 1949) John Ireland
I Was an American Spy (Allied Artists 1951) Ann Dvorak
I'll Be Seeing You (Selznick International 1945) Ginger Rogers
In Early Arizona (Columbia 1938) William Elliott
In Old Caliente (Republic 1939) Roy Rogers
In Old Cheyenne (Republic 1941) Roy Rogers
In Old Monterey (Republic 1939) Gene Autry
In Old Sacramento (Republic 1946) William Elliott
Indian Uprising (Columbia 1952) George Montgomery
Invisible Monster, The (Republic 1950) Richard Webb
Iron Claw, The (Columbia 1941) Charles Quigley
* Iron Horse, The (Fox 1924) George O'Brien
Iron Sheriff, The (United Artists 1957) Sterling Hayden
Jack Armstrong (Columbia 1947) John Hart
Jack Slade (Allied Artists 1953) Mark Stevens
Jackass Mail (MGM 1942) Wallace Beery
Jailbreakers, The (American International 1959) Robert Hutton
James Brothers of Missouri, The (Republic 1950) Keith Richards
Jesse James at Bay (Republic 1941) Roy Rogers
Jesse James Jr (Republic 1942) Donald Barry

Jesse James Rides Again (Republic 1947) Clayton Moore
Jiggs and Maggie Out West (Monogram 1950) Joe Yule and Renie Riano
Joe Palooka in Triple Cross (Monogram 1951) Joe Kirkwood
Johnny Concho (United Artists 1956) Frank Sinatra
Juarez (Warner Bros 1939) Paul Muni
Jungle Drums of Africa (Republic 1952) Clay Moore
Jungle Girl (Republic 1941) Frances Gifford
Jungle Menace (Columbia 1937) Frank Buck
Kansas Cyclone (Republic 1941) Donald Barry
Kansas Pacific (Allied Artists 1953) Sterling Hayden
Kansas Territory (Monogram 1952) William Elliott
Kansas Terrors, The (Republic 1939) Robert Livingston
Khyber Patrol (United Artists 1954) Richard Egan
Kid from Amarillo, The (Columbia 1951) Charles Starrett
Killer Leopard (Monogram 1954) John Sheffield
King of Dodge City (Columbia 1941) William Elliott
King of the Bandits (Monogram 1947) Gilbert Roland
King of the Bullwhip (Western Adventure 1951) Lash LaRue
King of the Congo (Columbia 1952) Buster Crabbe
King of the Cowboys (Republic 1943) Roy Rogers
King of the Forest Rangers (Republic 1946) Larry Thompson
King of the Jungle (Hercules 1927) Elmo Lincoln
King of the Jungle (Paramount 1933) Buster Crabbe
King of the Mounties (Republic 1942) Allan Lane
King of the Rocket Men (Republic 1949) Tristram Coffin
King of the Texas Rangers (Republic 1941) Sammy Baugh
King of the Wild Horses (Columbia 1947) Preston Foster
Kit Carson (United Artists 1940) Jon Hall
Land Beyond the Law (Warner Bros 1937) Dick Foran
Land of Fighting Men (Monogram 1938) Jack Randall
Landrush (Columbia 1946) Charles Starrett
Laramie (Columbia 1949) Charles Starrett
Laramie Mountains (Columbia 1952) Charles Starrett
Laramie Trail, The (Republic 1944) Robert Livingston
Last Bandit, The (Republic 1949) William Elliott
Last Frontier Uprising (Republic 1947) Monte Hale
Last Musketeer, The (Republic 1952) Rex Allen
Last of the Bad Men (Allied Artists 1957) George Montgomery
Last of the Clintons, The (Ajay 1935) Harry Carey
Last of the Mohicans, The (Mascot 1932) Harry Carey
Last of the Mohicans, The (United Artists 1936) Randolph Scott
Last of the Pony Riders (Columbia 1953) Gene Autry

Last Outlaw, The (RKO 1936) Harry Carey
Last Outpost, The (Paramount 1951) Ronald Reagan
Last Stagecoach West (Republic 1957) Jim Davis
Last Train from Madrid, The (Paramount 1937) Dorothy Lamour
Law and Lead (Colony 1936) Rex Bell
Law and Order (Universal 1940) Johnny Mack Brown
Law Comes to Texas, The (Columbia 1939) William Elliott
Law Men (Monogram 1944) Johnny Mack Brown
Law of the Badlands (RKO 1950) Tim Holt
Law of the Canyon (Columbia 1946) Charles Starrett
Law of the Golden West (Republic 1949) Monte Hale
Law of the Lash (PRC 1947) Lash LaRue
Law of the Lawless (Paramount 1964) Dale Robertson
Law of the Panhandle (Monogram 1950) Johnny Mack Brown
Law of the Range (Universal 1941) Johnny Mack Brown
Law of the Saddle (PRC 1943) Robert Livingston
Law of the Texan (Columbia 1938) Buck Jones
Law of the Wild, The (Mascot 1934) Rex King of the Wild Horses
Lawless Breed (Universal 1946) Kirby Grant
Lawless Cowboys (Monogram 1951) Whip Wilson
Lawless Eighties, The (Republic 1957) Buster Crabbe
Lawless Empire (Columbia 1945) Charles Starrett
Lawless Plainsmen (Columbia 1942) Charles Starrett
Lawless Rider, The (United Artists 1954) Johnny Carpenter
Lawless Riders (Columbia 1935) Ken Maynard
Lay That Rifle Down (Republic 1955) Judy Canova
Leadville Gunslinger (Republic 1952) Allan Lane
Legend of Tom Dooley, The (Columbia 1959) Michael Landon
Light of Western Stars, The (Paramount 1940) Russell Hayden
Lightnin' in the Forest (Republic 1948) Donald Barry
Lightning Guns (Columbia 1950) Charles Starrett
Lightning Raiders (PRC 1946)
Lightning Warrior, The (Mascot 1931) Rin-Tin-Tin
Lion's Den, The (Puritan 1936)
Little Big Horn (Lippert 1951) John Ireland
Lives of a Bengal Lancer, The (Paramount 1935) Gary Cooper
Loaded Pistols (Columbia 1949) Gene Autry
Lone Avenger, The (Fox 1933) Ken Maynard
Lone Gun, The (United Artists 1954) George Montgomery
Lone Prairie, The (Columbia 1946) Russell Hayden
Lone Ranger Rides Again, The (Republic 1939) Robert Livingston
Lone Ranger, The (Republic 1938) Lee Powell

Lone Ranger, The (Warner Bros 1956) Clayton Moore
Lone Rider Crosses the Rio, The (PRC 1941) George Houston
Lone Rider in Cheyenne, The (PRC 1942) George Houston
Lone Rider in Ghost Town, The (PRC 1941) George Houston
Lone Rider in Texas Justice, The (PRC 1942) George Houston
Lone Rider Rides On, The (PRC 1941) George Houston
Lone Star Pioneers (Columbia 1939) William Elliott
Lone Star Raiders (Republic 1940) Three Mesquiteers
Lone Star Vigilantes (Columbia 1942) William Elliott
Lone Texan (20th Century-Fox 1959) Willard Parker
Lone Texas Ranger (Republic 1945) William Elliott
Lonely Man, The (Paramount 1957) Jack Palance
Longhorn, The (Monogram 1951) William Elliott
Lost Planet, The (Columbia 1953) Judd Holdren
Luck of Roaring Camp, The (Monogram 1937) Owen Davis Jr.
Lucky Cisco Kid (20th Century-Fox 1940) Cesar Romero
Lucky Terror (Diversion 1936) Hoot Gibson
Lumberjack (United Artists 1944) William Boyd
Man-Woman-Marriage (Allen Holubar Pictures) Dorothy Phillips
Ma and Pa Kettle Back on the Farm (Universal 1951) Marjorie Main
Male and Female (Paramount 1919) Thomas Meighan
Man Behind the Gun, The (Warner Bros 1953) Randolph Scott
Man from Cheyenne (Republic 1942) Roy Rogers
Man from Colorado, The (Columbia 1948) Glenn Ford
Man from God's Country (Allied Artists 1958) George Montgomery
Man from Oklahoma (Republic 1945) Roy Rogers
Man From Rainbow Valley, The (Republic 1946) Monte Hale
Man From Sonora (Monogram 1951) Johnny Mack Brown
Man from the Black Hills (Monogram 1952) Johnny Mack Brown
Man from the Rio Grande, The (Republic 1943) Donald Barry
Man from Thunder River, The (Republic 1943) William Elliott
Man from Tumbleweeds, The (Columbia 1940) William Elliott
Man in the Saddle, The (Columbia 1951) Randolph Scott
Man of Conquest (Republic 1939) Richard Dix
Man Trailer, The (Columbia 1934) Buck Jones
Man with the Gun (United Artists 1955) Robert Mitchum
Man with the Steel Whip (Republic 1954) Richard Simmons
Mandrake the Magician (Columbia 1939) Warren Hull
Manhunt of Mystery Island (Republic 1945) Richard Bailey
Marauders, The (United Artists 1947) William Boyd
Mark of the Lash (Screen Guild 1948) Lash LaRue
Marksman, The (Allied Artists 1953) Wayne Morris

Marshal of Amarillo (Republic 1948) Allan Lane
Marshal of Cedar Rock (Republic 1953) Allan Lane
Marshal of Cripple Creek (Republic 1947) Allan Lane
Marshal of Heldorado (Lippert 1950) Jimmie Ellison
Marshal of Laredo (Republic 1945) William Elliott
Marshal of Reno (Republic 1944) William Elliott
Marshal's Daughter, The (United Artists 1953) Johnny Mack Brown
Mask of the Avenger (Columbia 1951) John Derek
Masked Rider, The (Universal 1941) Johnny Mack Brown
Massacre River (Allied Artists 1949) Guy Madison
Masterson of Kansas (Columbia 1954) George Montgomery
Maverick, The (Allied Artists 1952) William Elliott
Men of Texas (Universal 1942) Robert Stack
Mexican Hayride (Universal 1948) Abbott & Costello
Millerson Case, The (Columbia 1947) Warner Baxter
Million Dollar Dollies, The (Emerald 1918) Jenny Dolly
Miracle Rider, The (Mascot 1935) Tom Mix
Missouri Outlaw, A (Republic 1941) Donald Barry
Missourians, The (Republic 1950) Monte Hale
Mojave Firebrand (Republic 1944) William Elliott
Montana Desperado (Monogram 1951) Johnny Mack Brown
Montana Incident (Monogram 1952) Whip Wilson
Montana Moon (MGM 1930) Johnny Mack Brown
Montana Territory (Columbia 1952) Preston Foster
Morgan's Last Raid (MGM 1929) Tim McCoy
Morocco (Paramount 1930) Gary Cooper
Motorcycle Cheerleading Mommas (Timeless Mulimedia 1997) Christopher
Mitchum
Motorcycle Gang (American International 1957) Anne Neyland
Mountain Rhythm (Republic 1939) Gene Autry
Mule Train (Columbia 1950) Gene Autry
My Official Wife (Vitagraph 1914) Clara Kimball Young
My Pal Trigger (Republic 1946) Roy Rogers
Mysterious Desperado, The (Republic 1949) Tim Holt
Mysterious Doctor Satan (Republic 1940) Edward Ciannelli
Mysterious Island (Columbia 1951) Richard Crane
Mystery Man (United Artists 1944) William Boyd
Mystery Mountain (Mascot 1934) Ken Maynard
Mystic Warrior, The (Warner Bros 1984) Will Sampson
Naked Hills, The (Allied Artists 1956) David Wayne
Narrow Trail, The (Artcraft 1917) William S. Hart
Navajo Trail Raiders (Republic 1949) Allan Lane

Nevada Badmen (Monogram 1951) Whip Wilson
Nevada City (Republic 1941) Roy Rogers
Nevadan, The (Columbia 1950) Randolph Scott
New Mexico (United Artists 1951) Lew Ayres
Night Raiders (Monogram 1952) Whip Wilson
Night Riders of Montana (Republic 1951) Allan Lane
Night Stage to Galveston (Columbia 1952) Gene Autry
Night the World Exploded, The (Columbia 1957) Kathryn Grant
Nine Lives of Elfego Baca, The (Buena Vista 1958) Robert Loggia
Noah's Ark (Warner Bros 1928) George O'Brien
Noose for a Gunman (United Artists 1960) Jim Davis
North from the Lone Star (Columbia 1941) William Elliott
North of the Border (Screen Guild 1946) Russell Hayden
North of the Rockies (Columbia 1942) William Elliott
Oh! Susanna (Republic 1936) Gene Autry
Oklahoma Badlands (Republic 1948) Allan Lane
Oklahoma Justice (Monogram 1951) Johnny Mack Brown
Oklahoma Kid, The (Warner Bros 1939) James Cagney
Oklahoma Renegades (Republic 1940) Robert Livingston
Oklahoma Territory (United Artists 1960) Gloria Talbott
Oklahoman, The (United Artists 1957) Joel McCrea
Old Barn Dance, The (Republic 1938) Gene Autry
Old Corral, The (Republic 1936) Gene Autry
Old Frontier, The (Republic 1950) Monte Hale
Old Los Angeles (Republic 1948) William Elliott
Old Oklahoma Plains (Republic 1952) Rex Allen
Old Soak, The (MGM 1937) Wallace Beery
Old Texas Trail, The (Universal 1944) Rod Cameron
Old Wyoming Trail, The (Columbia 1937) Charles Starrett
Old Yeller (Buena Vista 1958) Fess Parker
Omaha Trail, The (MGM 1942) Dean Jagger
One Foot in Hell (20th Century-Fox 1960) Alan Ladd
One Man's Law (Republic 1940) Donald Barry
Oregon Trail (Republic 1945) Sunset Carson
Oregon Trail, The (20th Century-Fox 1959) Fred MacMurray
Out California Way (Republic 1946) Monte Hale
Outcasts of Black Mesa (Columbia 1950) Charles Starrett
Outcasts of Poker Flat, The (RKO 1937) Harry Carey
Outcasts of the Trail (Republic 1949) Monte Hale
Outlaw Country (Screen Guild 1949) Lash LaRue
Outlaw Deputy, The (Puritan 1935) Tim McCoy
Outlaw Express (Universal 1938) Bob Baker

Outlaw Gold (Monogram 1950) Johnny Mack Brown
Outlaw Justice (Majestic 1932) Jack Hoxie
Outlaw Stallion, The (Columbia 1954) Philip Carey
Outlaw Women (Lippert 1952) Marie Windsor
Outlaw's Son (United Artists 1957) Dane Clark
Outlaws of Boulder Pass (PRC 1942) George Houston
Outlaws of Pine Ridge (Republic 1942) Donald Barry
Outlaws of Santa Fe (Republic 1943) Don Red Barry
Outlaws of Sonora (Republic 1938) Three Mesquiteers
Outlaws of Stampede Pass (Monogram 1943) Johnny Mack Brown
Outlaws of Texas (Monogram 1950) Whip Wilson
Outlaws of the Panhandle (Columbia 1941) Charles Starrett
Outlaws of the Rockies (Columbia 1945) Charles Starrett
Over the Border (Monogram 1950) Johnny Mack Brown
Over the Santa Fe Trail (Columbia 1947) Ken Curtis
Overland Express, The (Columbia 1938) Buck Jones
Overland Mail Robbery (Republic 1943) William Elliott
Overland Pacific (United Artists 1954) Jack Mahoney
Overland Stage Raiders (Republic 1938) Three Mesquiteers
Overland Stagecoach (PRC 1942) Robert Livingston
Overland Telegraph (RKO 1951) Tim Holt
Overland to Deadwood (Columbia 1942) Charles Starrett
Overland Trails (Monogram 1948) Johnny Mack Brown
Ox-Bow Incident, The (20th Century Fox 1943) Henry Fonda
Pack Train (Columbia 1953) Gene Autry
Painted Stallion, The (Republic 1937) Ray Corrigan
Paleface, The (First National Pictures 1922) Buster Keaton
Pals of the Pecos (Republic 1941) Robert Livingston
Pals of the Prairie (Imperial 1934) Jay Wilsey
Pals of the Range (Superior 1935) Rex Lease
Pals of the West (Imperial 1934) Wally Wales
Panic In Year Zero! (American International 1962) Ray Milland
Pardners (Paramount 1956) Martin & Lewis
Pardon My Gun (Columbia 1942) Charles Starrett
Paroled—-to Die (Republic 1938) Bob Steele
Partners (RKO 1932) Tom Keene
Pecos River (Columbia 1951) Charles Starrett
Perils of Nyoka (Republic 1942) Kay Alridge
Perils of the Royal Mounted (Columbia 1942) Robert Stevens
Phantom Cowboy, The (Republic 1941) Donald Barry
Phantom of the Plains (Republic 1945) William Elliott
Phantom Plainsmen, The (Republic 1942) Three Mesquiteers

Phantom Ranger, The (Monogram 1938) Tim McCoy
Phantom Rider, The (Republic 1945) Robert Kent
Phantom Stagecoach, The (Columbia 1957) William Bishop
Phantom Valley (Columbia 1948) Charles Starrett
Phantom, The (Columbia 1941) Tom Tyler
Pinto Kid, The (Columbia 1941) Charles Starrett
Pinto Rustlers (Reliable 1936) Tom Tyler
Pioneer Days (Monogram 1940) Jack Randall
Pioneer Justice (PRC 1947) Lash LaRue
Pioneer Marshal (Republic 1949) Monte Hale
Pioneer Trail (Columbia 1938) Jack Luden
Pioneers of the Frontier (Columbia 1940) William Elliott
Pioneers of the West (Republic 1940) Robert Livingston
Pirates of the High Seas (Columbia 1950) Buster Crabbe
Pistol Harvest (RKO 1951) Tim Holt
Plainsman and the Lady, The (Republic 1946) William Elliott
Plainsman, The (Paramount 1936) Gary Cooper
Plunderers of Painted Flats (Republic 1958) John Carroll
Plunderers, The (Allied Artists 1960) Jeff Chandler
Plunderers, The (Republic 1948) Rod Cameron
Pony Post (Universal 1940) Johnny Mack Brown
Powder River Rustlers (Republic 1949) Allan Lane
Power and the Glory, The (Fox 1933) Spencer Tracy
Prairie Express (Monogram 1947) Johnny Mack Brown
Prairie Gunsmoke (Columbia 1942) William Elliott
Prairie Moon (Republic 1938) Gene Autry
Prairie Outlaws (PRC 1946) Eddie Dean
Prairie Pals (PRC 1942) Art Davis
Prairie Pioneers (Republic 1941) Robert Livingston
Prairie Roundup (Columbia 1951) Charles Starrett
Prairie Rustlers (PRC 1945) Buster Crabbe
Prairie Schooners (Columbia 1940) William Elliott
Prairie Thunder (Warner Bros 1937) Dick Foran
Pride of the Plains (Republic 1944) Robert Livingston
Prince of the Plains (Republic 1949) Monte Hale
Public Cowboy No. 1 (Republic 1937) Gene Autry
Purple Monster Strikes, The (Republic 1945) Dennis Moore
Purple Vigilantes, The (Republic 1938) Three Mesquiteers
Quantrill's Raiders (Allied Artists 1958) Steve Cochran
Quick Gun, The (Columbia 1964) Audie Murphy
Quick on the Trigger (Columbia 1948) Charles Starrett
Racketeers of the Range (RKO 1939) George O'Brien

Radar Men From the Moon (Republic 1951) George Wallace
Radar Patrol vs Spy King (Republic 1950) Kirk Alyn
Raid, The (20th Century-Fox 1954) Van Heflin
Raiders of Ghost City (Universal 1944) Dennis Moore
Raiders of Sunset Pass (Republic 1943) Eddie Dew
Raiders of the Range (Republic 1942) Bob Steele
Raiders of the South (Monogram 1947) Johnny Mack Brown
Raiders of the West (PRC 1942) Bill "Rambler" Boyd
Raiders of Tomahawk Creek (Columbia 1950) Charles Starrett
Rancho Grande (Republic 1940) Gene Autry
Rancho Notorious (RKO 1952) Marlene Dietrich
Range Beyond the Blue (PRC 1947) Eddie Dean
Range Busters, The (Monogram 1940) Range Busters
Range Defenders (Republic 1937) Three Mesquiteers
Range Riders (Superior 1934) Buddy Roosevelt
Range Warfare (Kent 1935) Reb Russell
Ranger Courage (Columbia 1937) Bob Allen
Ranger of Cherokee Strip (Republic 1949) Monte Hale
Rangers Take Over, The (PRC 1943) Dave (Tex) O'Brien
Rawhide Rangers (Universal 1941) Johnny Mack Brown
Rawhide Trail, The (Allied Artists 1958) Rex Reason
Real Glory, The (Goldwyn 1939) Gary Cooper
Rebel City (Allied Artists 1953) William Elliott
Rebellion (Crescent 1936) Tom Keene
Red Desert (Lippert 1949) Don Barry
Red Mountain (Paramount 1951) Alan Ladd
Red River (United Artists 1948) John Wayne
Red River Range (Republic 1938) Three Mesquiteers
Red River Renegades (Republic 1946) Sunset Carson
Red River Robin Hood (RKO 1943) Tim Holt
Red River Valley (Republic 1936) Gene Autry
Red River Valley (Republic 1941) Roy Rogers
Red Stallion, The (Eagle Lion 1947) Robert Page
Red Tomahawk (Paramount 1967) Howard Keel
Redhead and the Cowboy, The (Paramount 1951) Glenn Ford
Renegade Ranger, The (RKO 1938) George O'Brien
Renegades of the Rio Grande (Universal 1945) Rod Cameron
Renegades of the Sage (Columbia 1949) Charles Starrett
Renegades, The (Columbia 1946) Evelyn Keyes
Requiem for a Gunfighter (Embassy 1965) Rod Cameron
Return of Daniel Boone, The (Columbia 1941) William Elliott
Return of the Bad Men (RKO 1948) Randolph Scott

Return of the Frontiersman (Warner Bros 1950) Gordon MacRae
Return of the Lash (PRC 1947) Lash LaRue
Return of Wild Bill, The (Columbia 1940) William Elliott
Return to Warbow (Columbia 1958) Philip Carey
Rhythm of the Saddle (Republic 1938) Gene Autry
Richard the Lion-Hearted (Allied Producers 1923) Wallace Beery
Ride 'Em Cowboy (Universal 1942) Abbott & Costello
Ride Clear of Diablo (Universal 1953) Audie Murphy
Ride, Ryder, Ride (Eagle-Lion 1949) Jim Bannon
Riders in the Sky (Columbia 1949) Gene Autry
Riders of Black Mountain (PDC 1940) Tim McCoy
Riders of Death Valley (Universal 1941) Dick Foran
Riders of the Badlands (Columbia 1941) Charles Starrett
Riders of the Black Hills (Republic 1938) Three Mesquiteers
Riders of the Dusk (Monogram 1949) Whip Wilson
Riders of the Northland (Columbia 1942) Charles Starrett
Riders of the Rio Grande (Republic 1943) Bob Steele
Riders of the Whistling Skull (Republic 1937) Three Mesquiteers
Ridin' Down the Trail (Monogram 1947) Jimmy Wakely
Ridin' the Lone Trail (Republic 1937) Bob Steele
Ridin' the Outlaw Trail (Columbia 1951) Charles Starrett
Riding Shotgun (Warner Bros 1954) Randolph Scott
Riding Through Nevada (Columbia 1942) Charles Starrett
Riding Wild (Columbia 1935) Tim McCoy
Riding with Buffalo Bill (Columbia 1954) Marshall Reed
Rim of the Canyon (Columbia 1949) Gene Autry
Rimfire (Lippert 1949) James Millican
Rio Grande Patrol (RKO Radio 1950) Tim Holt
Rio Grande Raiders (Republic 1946) Sunset Carson
Rip Van Winkle (Ward Lascelle Productions 1921) Thomas Jefferson
Road Agent (RKO 1952) Tim Holt
Road Agent (Universal 1941) Dick Foran
Roarin' Lead (Republic 1936) Three Mesquiteers
Roaring Frontiers (Columbia 1941) William Elliott
Roaring Rangers (Columbia 1946) Charles Starrett
Roaring Six Guns (Ambassador 1937) Kermit Maynard
Robin Hood of Monterey (Monogram 1947) Gilbert Roland
Robin Hood of Texas (Republic 1947) Gene Autry
Rocky Mountain Rangers (Republic 1940) Three Mesquiteers
Rocky Rhodes (Universal 1934) Buck Jones
Rodeo Queen and the Senorita, The (Republic 1951) Rex Allen
Roll Along, Cowboy (20th Century-Fox 1937) Smith Ballew

Roll On, Texas Moon (Republic 1946) Roy Rogers
Roll, Thunder, Roll (Eagle Lion 1949) Jim Bannon
Rollin' Plains (Grand National 1938) Tex Ritter
Rolling Caravans (Columbia 1938) Jack Luden
Rolling Down the Great Divide (PRC 1942) Bill "Cowboy" Boyd
Romance of the Rio Grande (20th Century-Fox 1941) Cesar Romero
Romance of the Rockies (Monogram 1937) Tom Keene
Romance of the West (PRC 1946) Eddie Dean
Romance on the Range (Republic 1942) Roy Rogers
Rough Riders of Cheyenne (Republic 1945) Sunset Carson
Rough Riders of Durango (Republic 1950) Allan Lane
Rough Riders' Round-up (Republic 1939) Roy Rogers
Rough Ridin' Justice (Columbia 1945) Charles Starrett
Round-Up Time in Texas (Republic 1937) Gene Autry
Rustler's Paradise (Ajax 1935) Harry Carey
Rustler's Roundup (Universal 1946) Kirby Grant
Rustlers of Devil's Canyon (Republic 1947) Allan Lane
Rustlers of the Badlands (Columbia 1945) Charles Starrett
Rustlers on Horseback (Republic 1950) Allan Lane
Saddle Tramp (Universal 1950) Joel McCrea
Saddlemates (Republic 1941) Robert Livingston
Safari Drums (Monogram 1953) John Sheffield
Saga of Death Valley (Columbia 1939) Roy Rogers
Salt Lake Raiders (Republic 1950) Allan Lane
San Antone Ambush (Republic 1949) Monte Hale
San Antonio Kid, The (Republic 1944) William Elliott
San Fernando Valley (Republic 1944) Roy Rogers
Santa Fe (Columbia 1951) Randolph Scott
Santa Fe Saddlemates (Republic 1945) Sunset Carson
Santa Fe Scouts (Republic 1943) Bob Steele
Santa Fe Uprising (Republic 1946) Allan Lane
Savage Frontier (Republic 1953) Allan Lane
Savage Horde, The (Republic 1950) William Elliott
Scarlet Horseman, The (Universal 1946) Paul Guilfoyle
Sea of Grass, The (MGM 1947) Spencer Tracy
Secret of Treasure Island, The (Columbia 1938) Don Terry
Secret of Treasure Mountain (Columbia 1956) Raymond Burr
Secret Service in Darkest Africa (Republic 1943) Rod Cameron
Seminole Uprising (Columbia 1955) George Montgomery
Sequoia (MGM 1934) Jean Parker
Seven Guns to Mesa (Allied Artists 1958) Charles Quinlivan
Shadow Valley (Eagle Lion 1947) Eddie Dean

Shadows of the Sage (Republic 1942) Bob Steele
Sheriff of Cimarron (Republic 1945) Sunset Carson
Sheriff of Las Vegas (Republic 1944) William Elliott
Sheriff of Redwood Valley (Republic 1946) William Elliott
Sheriff of Sundown (Republic 1941) Allan Lane
Sheriff of Wichita (Republic 1949) Allan Lane
Shooting High (20th Century-Fox 1940) Gene Autry
Showdown, The (Republic 1950) William Elliott
Shut My Big Mouth (Columbia 1942) Joe E. Brown
Sierra Stranger (Columbia 1957) Howard Duff
Silent Man, The (Ince 1917) William S. Hart
Silver Canyon (Republic 1951) Gene Autry
Silver City Bonanza (Republic 1951) Rex Allen
Silver City Kid (Republic 1944) Allan Lane
Silver Raiders (Monogram 1950) Whip Wilson
Silver Spurs (Republic 1943) Roy Rogers
Silver Spurs (Universal 1936) Buck Jones
Silver Trails (Monogram 1948) Jimmy Wakely
Silver Treasure, The (Fox 1926) George O'Brien
Singin' in the Corn (Columbia 1946) Judy Canova
Singing Cowboy, The (Republic 1936) Gene Autry
Six-Gun Gold (RKO 1941) Tim Holt
Six-Gun Gospel (Monogram 1943) Johnny Mack Brown
Six-Gun Law (Buena Vista 1963) Robert Loggia
Six-Gun Man (PRC 1946) Bob Steele
Six-Gun Serenade (Monogram 1947) Jimmy Wakely
Six-Gun Trail (Victory 1938) Tim McCoy
Slave Girl, The (Reliance 1915) Elmo Lincoln
Slave Girl (Universal 1947) Yvonne De Carlo
Smokey Smith (Commodore 1935) Bob Steele
Smoky Canyon (Columbia 1951) Charles Starrett
Snake River Desperados (Columbia 1941) Charles Starrett
Sombrero Kid, The (Republic 1942) Donald Barry
Son of Bad Man (Screen Guild 1949) Lash LaRue
Son of Belle Starr (Allied Artists 1953) Keith Larsen
Son of Billy the Kid (Screen Guild 1949) Lash LaRue
Son of Davy Crockett, The (Columbia 1941) Bill Elliott
Son of Geronimo (Columbia 1952) Clayton Moore
Son of God's Country (Republic 1948) Monte Hale
Son of Paleface (Paramount 1952) Bob Hope
Son of Zorro (Republic 1947) George Turner
Song of Arizona (Republic 1946) Roy Rogers

Song of the Saddle (Warner Bros 1936) Dick Foran
Song of the Trail (Ambassador 1936) Kermit Maynard
Sons of New Mexico (Columbia 1949) Gene Autry
Sons of the Pioneers (Republic 1942) Roy Rogers
South of Death Valley (Columbia 1949) Charles Starrett
South of Monterey (Monogram 1946) Gilbert Roland
South of Rio (Republic 1949) Monte Hale
South of Santa Fe (Republic 1942) Roy Rogers
South of the Rio Grande (Columbia 1932) Buck Jones
Spoilers of the Plains (Republic 1951) Roy Rogers
Springfield Rifle (Warner Bros 1952) Gary Cooper
Spy Smasher (Republic 1942) Kane Richmond
Square Dance Jubilee (Lippert 1949) Donald Barry
Squaw Man, The (MGM 1931) Lupe Velez
Stage to Blue River (Monogram 1951) Whip Wilson
Stage to Mesa City (PRC 1947) Lash LaRue
Stage to Tucson (Columbia 1950) Rod Cameron
Stagecoach (United Artists 1939) John Wayne
Stagecoach Buckaroo (Universal 1942) Johnny Mack Brown
Stagecoach Days (Columbia 1938) Jack Luden
Stagecoach Driver (Monogram 1951) Whip Wilson
Stagecoach Express (Republic 1942) Donald Barry
Stagecoach to Denver (Republic 1946) Allan Lane
Stagecoach to Monterey (Republic 1944) Allan Lane
Stampede (Allied Artists 1949) Rod Cameron
Star of Texas (Allied Artists 1953) Wayne Morris
State Department: File 649 (Sigmund Neufeld Pictures 1949) William Lundigan
Stolen Ranch, The (Universal 1926) Fred Humes
Storm Over Bengal (Republic 1938) Patric Knowles
Storm Rider, The (20th Century-Fox 1957) Scott Brady
Stormy Trails (Colony 1936) Rex Bell
Story of G. I. Joe, The (Cowan Productions 1945) Burgess Meredith
Stranger From Pecos, The (Monogram 1943) Johnny Mack Brown
Stranger from Ponca City, The (Columbia 1947) Charles Starrett
Stranger Wore a Gun, The (Columbia 1953) Randolph Scott
Streets of Ghost Town (Columbia 1950) Charles Starrett
Sudden Death (Lippert 1950) Jimmy Ellison, Russ Hayden
Sun Valley Cyclone (Republic 1946) William Elliott
Sundown in Santa Fe (Republic 1948) Allan Lane
Sundown Kid, The (Republic 1942) Donald Barry
Sundown Valley (Columbia 1944) Charles Starrett
Sunset in El Dorado (Republic 1945) Roy Rogers

Sunset Trail, The (Tiffany 1932) Ken Maynard
Superman (Columbia 1948) Kirk Alyn
Support Your Local Sheriff (United Artists 1968) James Garner
Susanna Pass (Republic 1949) Roy Rogers
Tall Man Riding (Warner Bros 1955) Randolph Scott
Tall Texan, The (Lippert 1953) Lloyd Bridges
Taming of the West, The (Columbia 1939) William Elliott
Target (RKO 1952) Tim Holt
Tarzan and the Slave Girl (RKO 1950) Lex Barker
Tarzan the Ape Man (MGM 1932) Johnny Weissmuller
Tarzan the Fearless (Principal Productions 1933) Buster Crabbe
Tarzan's Peril (RKO 1951) Lex Barker
Tarzan's Savage Fury (RKO 1952) Lex Barker
Tarzan's Secret Treasure (MGM 1941) Johnny Weissmuller
Teenage Cave Man (American International 1958) Robert Vaughn
Teenage Monster (Marquette Productions 1958) Anne Gwynne
Tell It to the Marines (MGM 1926) Lon Chaney
Ten Tall Men (Columbia 1951) Burt Lancaster
Tenderfoot, The (First National 1932) Joe E. Brown
Tennessee's Partner (RKO 1955) John Payne
Tension at Table Rock (RKO 1956) Richard Egan
Tenting Tonight on the Old Camp Ground (Universal 1943) Johnny Mack Brown
Terror Trail (Columbia 1946) Charles Starrett
Terry and the Pirates (Columbia 1940) William Tracy
Texan Meets Calamity Jane, The (Columbia 1950) James Ellison
Texan, The (Principal 1932) Buffalo Bill Jr
Texans Never Cry (Columbia 1951) Gene Autry
Texas City (Monogram 1952) Johnny Mack Brown
Texas Cyclone (Columbia 1932) Tim McCoy
Texas Dynamo (Columbia 1950) Charles Starrett
Texas Justice (PRC 1942) George Houston
Texas Kid, The (Monogram 1943) Johnny Mack Brown
Texas Lawmen (Monogram 1951) Johnny Mack Brown
Texas Manhunt (PRC 1942) Lee Powell
Texas Panhandle (Columbia 1945) Charles Starrett
Texas Rangers, The (Columbia 1951) George Montgomery
Texas Stagecoach (Columbia 1940) Charles Starrett
Texas Terrors (Republic 1940) Donald Barry
Texas Wildcats (Victory 1939) Tim McCoy
They Died With Their Boots On (Warner Bros 1941) Errol Flynn
They Gave Him a Gun (MGM 1937) Spencer Tracy
They Rode West (Columbia 1954) Robert Francis

Thirty-Four Foot Bride of Candy Rock, The (Columbia 1959) Lou Costello
Three Ages (Metro 1923) Buster Keaton
Three Stooges Meet Hercules, The (Columbia 1962) Three Stooges
Three Word Brand (Paramount 1921) William S. Hart
Thunder in God's Country (Republic 1951) Rex Allen
Thunder in the Desert (Republic 1938) Bob Steele
Thunder Over Arizona (Republic 1956) Wallace Ford
Thunder Over Prairie (Columbia 1941) Charles Starrett
Thunder River Feud (Monogram 1942) Range Busters
Thunder Town (PRC 1946) Bob Steele
Thundering Caravans (Republic 1952) Rocky Lane
Thundering Hoofs (RKO 1942) Tim Holt
Thundering Trail, The (Western Adventure 1951) Lash LaRue
Thundering Trails (Republic 1943) Three Mesquiteers
Thundering West, The (Columbia 1939) Charles Starrett
Tiger Man, The (Artcraft 1918) William S. Hart
Timber Trail, The (Republic 1948) Monte Hale
Tobor the Great (Republic 1954) Charles Drake
Toll of the Desert (Commodore 1935) Fred Kohler Jr
Tomb, The (International Home Video 1986) Cameron Mitchell
Tomstone, the Town Too Tough to Die (Paramount 1942) Richard Dix
Tonto Kid, The (Resolute 1935) Rex Bell
Too Much Beef (Colony 1936) Rex Bell
Top Gun (United Artists 1955) Sterling Hayden
Topeka (Allied Artists 1953) William Elliott
Topeka Terror, The (Republic 1945) Allan Lane
Tornado in the Saddle, A (Columbia 1942) Russell Hayden
Tornado Range (Eagle Lion 1948) Eddie Dean
Tough Assignment (Lippert 1949) Donald Barry
Tougher They Come, The (Columbia 1950) Wayne Morris
Toughest Gun in Tombstone (United Artists 1958) George Montgomery
Tracked by the Police (Warner Bros 1927) Rin Tin Tin
Trader Tom of the China Seas (Republic 1954) Harry Lauter
Trail Blazers, The (Republic 1940) Robert Livingston
Trail Guide (RKO 1952) Tim Holt
Trail of Kit Carson (Republic 1945) Allan Lane
Trail of Robin Hood (Republic 1950) Roy Rogers
Trail of the Lonesome Pine, The (Paramount 1936) Henry Fonda
Trail of the Rustlers (Columbia 1950) Charles Starrett
Trail of the Vigilantes (Universal 1940) Franchot Tone
Trail of Vengeance (Republic 1937) Johnny Mack Brown
Trail to Laredo (Columbia 1948) Charles Starrett

Trailin' Trouble (Grand National 1937) Ken Maynard
Trailin' West (Warner Bros 1936) Dick Foran
Trailing Danger (Monogram 1947) Johnny Mack Brown
Trailing Double Trouble (Monogram 1940) Range Busters
Trailing Trouble (Grand National 1937) Ken Maynard
Train to Tombstone (Lippert 1950) Donald Barry
Traveling Saleslady, The (Columbia 1950) Joan Davis
Trigger Fingers (Victory 1939) Tim McCoy
Trigger Law (Monogram 1944) Hoot Gibson
Trigger Trail (Universal 1944) Rod Cameron
Triggerman (Monogram 1948) Johnny Mack Brown
Triple Justice (RKO 1940) George O'Brien
Trusted Outlaw, The (Republic 1937) Bob Steele
Tucson Raiders (Republic 1944) William Elliott
Tulsa Kid, The (Republic 1940) Donald Barry
Twilight in the Sierras (Republic 1950) Roy Rogers
Two Gun Law (Columbia 1937) Charles Starrett
Two Guns and a Badge (Allied Artists 1954) Wayne Morris
Two-Gun Sheriff (Republic 1941) Donald Barry
Under Arizona Skies (Monogram 1946) Johnny Mack Brown
Under Colorado Skies (Republic 1947) Monte Hale
Under Fiesta Stars (Republic 1941) Gene Autry
Under Texas Skies (Republic 1940) Three Mesquiteers
Under Texas Skies (Syndicate 1930) Bob Custer
Under the Tonto Rim (Paramount 1928) Richard Arlen
Under Western Skies (Universal 1945) Martha O'Driscoll
Undercover Man (United Artists 1942) William Boyd
Undercover Woman, The (Republic 1946) Stephanie Bachelor
Underground Rustlers (Monogram 1941) Range Busters
Undersea Kingdom (Republic 1936) Ray (Crash) Corrigan
Unknown Valley (Columbia 1933) Buck Jones
Untamed Breed (Columbia 1948) Barbara Britton
Untamed Heiress (Republic 1954) Judy Canova
Utah (Republic 1945) Roy Rogers
Utah Kid, The (Tiffany 1930) Rex Lease
Utah Trail (Grand National 1937) Tex Ritter
Utah Wagon Train (Republic 1951) Rex Allen
Vacation in Reno (RKO 1946) Jack Haley
Valerie (United Artists 1957) Sterling Hayden
Valiant Hombre, The (United Artists 1949) Duncan Renaldo
Valley of Hunted Men (Republic 1942) Three Mesquiteers
Valley of Terror (Ambassador 1937) Kermit Maynard

Valley of Vanishing Men, The (Columbia 1942) Bill Elliott
Vanishing Outpost, The (Western Adventure 1951) Lash LaRue
Vanishing Riders, The (Spectrum 1935) Bill Cody
Vanishing Westerner, The (Republic 1950) Monte Hale
Vengeance of the West (Columbia 1942) William Elliott
Vigilante Hideout (Republic 1950) Allan Lane
Vigilante Terror (Allied Artists 1953) William Elliott
Vigilante, Fighting Hero of the West (Columbia 1947) Ralph Byrd
Vigilantes Are Coming, The (Republic 1936) Robert Livingston
Vigilantes of Boomtown (Republic 1947) Allan Lane
Vigilantes of Dodge City (Republic 1944) Wild Bill Elliott
Vigilantes Return, The (Universal 1947) Jon Hall
Viking Women and the Sea Serpent (American International 1957) Abby Dalton
Virginian, The (Paramount 1929) Gary Cooper
Virginian, The (Paramount 1946) Joel McCrea
Voodoo Tiger (Columbia 1952) John Weissmuller
Waco (Monogram 1952) William Elliott
Wagon Team (Columbia 1952) Gene Autry
Wagon Tracks West (Republic 1943) William Elliott
Wagon Train (RKO 1940) Tim Holt
Wagon Wheels Westward (Republic 1945) William Elliott
Wagons Westward (Republic 1940) Buck Jones
Wall Street Cowboy (Republic 1939) Roy Rogers
Wanderers of the West (Monogram 1941) Tom Keene
Wanted: Dead or Alive (Monogram 1951) Whip Wilson
War of the Colossal Beast (American International 1957) Sally Fraser
Wee Willie Winkie (20th Century Fox 1937) Shirley Temple
Wells Fargo (Paramount 1937) Joel McCrea
Wells Fargo Gunmaster (Republic 1951) Allan Lane
West of Carson City (Universal 1940) Johnny Mack Brown
West of Cimarron (Republic 1942) Bob Steele
West of Dodge City (Columbia 1947) Charles Starrett
West of Sonora (Columbia 1948) Charles Starrett
West of Texas (PRC 1943) Texas Rangers
West of the Brazos (Lippert 1950) Jimmy Ellison
West of Tombstone (Columbia 1942) Charles Starrett
West of Wyoming (Monogram 1950) Johnny Mack Brown
West to Glory (PRC 1947) Eddie Dean
Western Caravans (Columbia 1939) Charles Starrett
Western Code, The (Columbia 1932) Tim McCoy
Western Courage (Columbia 1935) Ken Maynard
Western Cyclone (PRC 1943) Buster Crabbe

Western Jamboree (Republic 1938) Gene Autry
Western Trails (Universal 1938) Bob Baker
Westward Ho (Republic 1942) Bob Steele
Westward Trail, The (PRC 1948) Eddie Dean
When the Daltons Rode (Universal 1940) Randolph Scott
Whirlwind Horseman (Grand National 1938) Ken Maynard
Whistlin' Dan (Tiffany 1932) Ken Maynard
Whistling Hills (Monogram 1951) Johnny Mack Brown
White Eagle (Columbia 1941) Buck Jones
White Squaw, The (Columbia 1956) David Brian
Wild Beauty (Universal 1946) Don Porter, Dick Curtis
Wild Bill Hickock Rides (Warner Bros 1942) Bruce Cabot
Wild Country (PRC 1947) Eddie Dean
Wild Dakotas, The (Associated Film 1956) Bill Williams
Wild Frontier, The (Republic 1947) Allan Lane
Wild Gold (Fox 1934) John Boles
Wild Horse Ambush (Republic 1952) Michael Chapin
Wild Horse Phantom (PRC 1944) Buster Crabbe
Wild Horse Rodeo (Republic 1937) Three Mesquiteers
Wild Horse Roundup (Ambassador 1936) Kermit Maynard
Wild Horse Rustlers (PRC 1943) Robert Livingston
Wild Stallion (Monogram 1952) Ben Johnson
Wild West (PRC 1946) Eddie Dean
Wild Westerners, The (Columbia 1962) James Philbrook
Wildcat of Tucson (Columbia 1940) William Elliott
Winning of the West (Columbia 1953) Gene Autry
Wistful Widow of Wagon Gap, The (Universal 1947) Abbott & Costello
Wolves of the Range (PRC 1943) Robert Livingston
World Without End (Allied Artists 1956) Hugh Marlowe
Wyoming (Republic 1947) William Elliott
Wyoming Bandit, The (Republic 1949) Allan Lane
Wyoming Renegades (Columbia 1955) Philip Carey
Wyoming Roundup (Monogram 1952) Whip Wilson
Wyoming Wildcat (Republic 1941) Donald Barry
Yaqui Drums (Allied Artists 1956) Rod Cameron
Yellow Rose of Texas (Republic 1944) Roy Rogers
Young Buffalo Bill (Republic 1940) Roy Rogers
Young Eagles (Romance Productions 1934) Carter Dixon
Young Rajah, The (Paramount 1922) Rudolph Valentino
Younger Brothers, The (Warner Bros 1949) Wayne Morris
Zombies of the Stratosphere (Republic 1952) Judd Holdren
Zorro Rides Again (Republic 1937) John Carroll

Zorro's Black Whip (Republic 1944) Linda Stirling
Zorro's Fighting Legion (Republic 1939) Reed Hadley

SORTED BY YEAR

1914
My Official Wife (Vitagraph) Clara Kimball Young

1915
Slave Girl, The (Reliance) Elmo Lincoln

1917
Narrow Trail, The (Artcraft) William S. Hart
Silent Man, The (Ince) William S. Hart

1918
Million Dollar Dollies, The (Emerald) Jenny Dolly
Tiger Man, The (Artcraft) William S. Hart

1919
Elmo, the Mighty (Universal) Elmo Lincoln
Male and Female (Paramount) Thomas Meighan

1920
A Double-Dyed Deceiver (Goldwyn) Jack Pickford
Desert Love (Fox) Tom Mix

1921
Man-Woman-Marriage (Allen Holubar Pictures) Dorothy Phillips
Rip Van Winkle (Ward Lascelle Productions) Thomas Jefferson
Three Word Brand (Paramount) William S. Hart

1922
Do and Dare (Fox) Tom Mix
Paleface, The (First National Pictures) Buster Keaton
Young Rajah, The (Paramount) Rudolph Valentino

1923
Balloonatic, The (Metro) Buster Keaton
Covered Wagon, The (Paramount) J. Warren Kerrigan
Richard the Lion-Hearted (Allied Producers) Wallace Beery
Three Ages (Metro) Buster Keaton

1924
* Iron Horse, The (Fox) George O'Brien

1925
Ben Hur: A Tale of the Christ (MGM) Ramon Navarro
Clash of the Wolves (Warner Bros) Rin Tin Tin

1926
Devil Horse, The (Hal Roach) Rex the Wonder Horse
Silver Treasure, The (Fox) George O'Brien
Stolen Ranch, The (Universal) Fred Humes
Tell It to the Marines (MGM) Lon Chaney

1927
Gaucho, The (United Artists) Mary Pickford
King of the Jungle (Hercules) Elmo Lincoln
Tracked by the Police (Warner Bros) Rin Tin Tin

1928
Flying Elephants (Roach) Laurel and Hardy
Noah's Ark (Warner Bros) George O'Brien
Under the Tonto Rim (Paramount) Richard Arlen

1929
Black Watch, The (Fox) Victor McLaglen
Morgan's Last Raid (MGM) Tim McCoy
Virginian, The (Paramount) Gary Cooper

1930
Arizona Kid, The (20th Century-Fox) Carol Lombard
Green Goddess, The (Warner Bros) George Arliss
Montana Moon (MGM) Johnny Mack Brown
Morocco (Paramount) Gary Cooper
Under Texas Skies (Syndicate) Bob Custer
Utah Kid, The (Tiffany) Rex Lease

1931
Branded (Columbia) Buck Jones
Cisco Kid, The (Fox) Warner Baxter
Fighting Sheriff, The (Columbia) Buck Jones
Freighters of Destiny (RKO Pathe) Tom Keene
Hurricane Horseman (Kent) Lane Chandler
Lightning Warrior, The (Mascot) Rin-Tin-Tin
Squaw Man, The (MGM) Lupe Velez

1932

Come On, Danger (Radio Pictures) Tom Keene
Cornered (Columbia) Tim McCoy
Devil Horse, The (Mascot) Harry Carey
Flaming Guns (Universal) Tom Mix
Fourth Horseman, The (Universal) Tom Mix
Last of the Mohicans, The (Mascot) Harry Carey
Outlaw Justice (Majestic) Jack Hoxie
Partners (RKO) Tom Keene
South of the Rio Grande (Columbia) Buck Jones
Sunset Trail, The (Tiffany) Ken Maynard
Tarzan the Ape Man (MGM) Johnny Weissmuller
Tenderfoot, The (First National) Joe E. Brown
Texan, The (Principal) Buffalo Bill Jr
Texas Cyclone (Columbia) Tim McCoy
Western Code, The (Columbia) Tim McCoy
Whistlin' Dan (Tiffany) Ken Maynard

1933

California Trail, The (Columbia) Buck Jones
Cheyenne Kid, The (Radio) Tom Keene
Fargo Express (Fox) Ken Maynard
Fighting With Kit Carson (Mastoc) Johnny Mack Brown
Gun Law (Majestic) Jack Hoxie
King of the Jungle (Paramount) Buster Crabbe
Lone Avenger, The (Fox) Ken Maynard
Power and the Glory, The (Fox) Spencer Tracy
Tarzan the Fearless (Principal Productions) Buster Crabbe
Unknown Valley (Columbia) Buck Jones

1934

Behold My Wife! (Paramount) Sylvia Sidney
Dude Ranger, The (Fox) George O'Brien
Fighting Through (Kent) Reb Russell
Law of the Wild, The (Mascot) Rex King of the Wild Horses
Man Trailer, The (Columbia) Buck Jones
Mystery Mountain (Mascot) Ken Maynard
Pals of the Prairie (Imperial) Jay Wilsey
Pals of the West (Imperial) Wally Wales
Range Riders (Superior) Buddy Roosevelt
Rocky Rhodes (Universal) Buck Jones
Sequoia (MGM) Jean Parker

Wild Gold (Fox) John Boles
Young Eagles (Romance Productions) Carter Dixon

1935
Annie Oakley (RKO) Barbara Stanwyck
Arizonian, The (RKO) Richard Dix
Bar 20 Rides Again (Paramount) William Boyd
Blazing Guns (Kent) Reb Russell
Cyclone Ranger, The (Spectrum) Bill Cody
Dawn Rider, The (Monogram) John Wayne
Gilded Lily, The (Paramount) Claudette Colbert
Gunfire (Resolute) Rex Bell
Heir to Trouble (Columbia) Ken Maynard
Last of the Clintons, The (Ajay) Harry Carey
Lawless Riders (Columbia) Ken Maynard
Lives of a Bengal Lancer, The (Paramount) Gary Cooper
Miracle Rider, The (Mascot) Tom Mix
Outlaw Deputy, The (Puritan) Tim McCoy
Pals of the Range (Superior) Rex Lease
Range Warfare (Kent) Reb Russell
Riding Wild (Columbia) Tim McCoy
Rustler's Paradise (Ajax) Harry Carey
Smokey Smith (Commodore) Bob Steele
Toll of the Desert (Commodore) Fred Kohler Jr
Tonto Kid, The (Resolute) Rex Bell
Vanishing Riders, The (Spectrum) Bill Cody
Western Courage (Columbia) Ken Maynard

1936
Avenging Waters (Columbia) Ken Maynard
Big Show, The (Republic) Gene Autry
Bold Caballero, The (Republic) Robert Livingston
California Mail, The (Warner Bros) Dick Foran
Cavalcade of the West (Grand National) Hoot Gibson
Charge of the Light Brigade, The (Warner Bros) Errol Flynn
Country Beyond, The (20th Century-Fox) Rochelle Hudson
Cowboy Star, The (Columbia) Charles Starrett
Custer's Last Stand (Weiss Productions) Rex Lease
Daniel Boone (RKO) George O'Brien
Darkest Africa (Republic) Clyde Beatty
Desert Gold (Paramount) Buster Crabbe
Desire (Paramount) Gary Cooper

Fast Bullets (Reliable) Tom Tyler
Fugitive Sheriff, The (Columbia) Ken Maynard
Garden of Allah, The (Selznick) Marlene Dietrich
Ghost Town Gold (Republic) Three Mesquiteers
Glory Trail, The (Crescent) Tom Keene
Last of the Mohicans, The (United Artists) Randolph Scott
Last Outlaw, The (RKO) Harry Carey
Law and Lead (Colony) Rex Bell
Lion's Den, The (Puritan)
Lucky Terror (Diversion) Hoot Gibson
Oh! Susanna (Republic) Gene Autry
Old Corral, The (Republic) Gene Autry
Pinto Rustlers (Reliable) Tom Tyler
Plainsman, The (Paramount) Gary Cooper
Rebellion (Crescent) Tom Keene
Red River Valley (Republic) Gene Autry
Roarin' Lead (Republic) Three Mesquiteers
Silver Spurs (Universal) Buck Jones
Singing Cowboy, The (Republic) Gene Autry
Song of the Saddle (Warner Bros) Dick Foran
Song of the Trail (Ambassador) Kermit Maynard
Stormy Trails (Colony) Rex Bell
Too Much Beef (Colony) Rex Bell
Trail of the Lonesome Pine, The (Paramount) Henry Fonda
Trailin' West (Warner Bros) Dick Foran
Undersea Kingdom (Republic) Ray (Crash) Corrigan
Vigilantes Are Coming, The (Republic) Robert Livingston
Wild Horse Roundup (Ambassador) Kermit Maynard

1937
Blazing Sixes (Warner Bros) Dick Foran
Ali Baba Goes to Town (20th Century-Fox) Eddie Cantor
Bar Z Bad Men (Republic) Johnny Mack Brown
Bride Wore Red, The (MGM) Joan Crawford
Californian, The (20th Century-Fox) Ricardo Cortez
Cherokee Flash, The (Republic) Sunset Carson
Cherokee Strip, The (Warner Bros) Dick Foran
Cheyenne Rides Again (Victory) Tom Tyler
Come On, Cowboys (Republic) Three Mesquiteers
Doomed at Sundown (Republic) Bob Steele
Empty Holsters (Warner Bros) Dick Foran
Fighting Texan, The (Ambassador) Kermit Maynard

Firefly, The (MGM) Jeanette MacDonald
Gambling Terror, The (Republic) Johnny Mack Brown
Git Along Little Doggies (Republic) Gene Autry
19Guns in the Dark (Republic) Johnny Mack Brown
Guns of the Pecos (Warner Bros) Dick Foran
Gunsmoke Ranch (Republic) Three Mesquiteers
Heart of the Rockies (Republic) Three Mesquiteers
High, Wide and Handsome (Paramount) Irene Dunne
Hit the Saddle (Republic) Three Mesquiteers
Hi-Yo Silver (Republic) Lee Powell
Jungle Menace (Columbia) Frank Buck
Land Beyond the Law (Warner Bros) Dick Foran
Last Train from Madrid, The (Paramount) Dorothy Lamour
Luck of Roaring Camp, The (Monogram) Owen Davis Jr.
Old Soak, The (MGM) Wallace Beery
Old Wyoming Trail, The (Columbia) Charles Starrett
Outcasts of Poker Flat, The (RKO) Harry Carey
Painted Stallion, The (Republic) Ray Corrigan
Prairie Thunder (Warner Bros) Dick Foran
Public Cowboy No. 1 (Republic) Gene Autry
Range Defenders (Republic) Three Mesquiteers
Ranger Courage (Columbia) Bob Allen
Riders of the Whistling Skull (Republic) Three Mesquiteers
Ridin' the Lone Trail (Republic) Bob Steele
Roaring Six Guns (Ambassador) Kermit Maynard
Roll Along, Cowboy (20th Century-Fox) Smith Ballew
Romance of the Rockies (Monogram) Tom Keene
Round-Up Time in Texas (Republic) Gene Autry
They Gave Him a Gun (MGM) Spencer Tracy
Trail of Vengeance (Republic) Johnny Mack Brown
Trailin' Trouble (Grand National) Ken Maynard
Trailing Trouble (Grand National) Ken Maynard
Trusted Outlaw, The (Republic) Bob Steele
Two Gun Law (Columbia) Charles Starrett
Utah Trail (Grand National) Tex Ritter
Valley of Terror (Ambassador) Kermit Maynard
Wee Willie Winkie (20th Century Fox) Shirley Temple
Wells Fargo (Paramount) Joel McCrea
Wild Horse Rodeo (Republic) Three Mesquiteers
Zorro Rides Again (Republic) John Carroll

1938

Army Girl (Republic) Madge Evans
Billy the Kid Returns (Republic) Roy Rogers
Black Bandit, The (Universal) Bob Baker
Call of the Rockies (Columbia) Charles Starrett
Call the Mesquiteers (Republic) Three Mesquiteers
Come On, Leathernecks! (Republic) Richard Cromwell
Come On, Rangers (Republic) Roy Rogers
Cowboy and the Lady, The (United Artists) Gary Cooper
Durango Valley Raiders (Republic) Bob Steele
Feud Maker, The (Republic) Bob Steele
Fighting Gringo, The (RKO) George O'Brien
Flight Into Nowhere (Columbia) Jack Holt
Ghost Town Riders (Universal) Bob Baker
Great Adventures of Wild Bill Hickok, The (Columbia) William Elliott
Gunsmoke Trail (Monogram) Jack Randall
Hawk of the Wilderness (Republic) Herman Brix
In Early Arizona (Columbia) William Elliott
Land of Fighting Men (Monogram) Jack Randall
Law of the Texan (Columbia) Buck Jones
Lone Ranger, The (Republic) Lee Powell
Old Barn Dance, The (Republic) Gene Autry
Outlaw Express (Universal) Bob Baker
Outlaws of Sonora (Republic) Three Mesquiteers
Overland Express, The (Columbia) Buck Jones
Overland Stage Raiders (Republic) Three Mesquiteers
Paroled—-to Die (Republic) Bob Steele
Phantom Ranger, The (Monogram) Tim McCoy
Pioneer Trail (Columbia) Jack Luden
Prairie Moon (Republic) Gene Autry
Purple Vigilantes, The (Republic) Three Mesquiteers
Red River Range (Republic) Three Mesquiteers
Renegade Ranger, The (RKO) George O'Brien
Rhythm of the Saddle (Republic) Gene Autry
Riders of the Black Hills (Republic) Three Mesquiteers
Rollin' Plains (Grand National) Tex Ritter
Rolling Caravans (Columbia) Jack Luden
Secret of Treasure Island, The (Columbia) Don Terry
Six-Gun Trail (Victory) Tim McCoy
Stagecoach Days (Columbia) Jack Luden
Storm Over Bengal (Republic) Patric Knowles
Thunder in the Desert (Republic) Bob Steele

Western Jamboree (Republic) Gene Autry
Western Trails (Universal) Bob Baker
Whirlwind Horseman (Grand National) Ken Maynard

1939
Adventures of the Masked Phantom, The (Equity) Monte Rawlins
Arizona Kid, The (Republic) Roy Rogers
Arizona Legion (RKO) George O'Brien
Calling All Marines (Republic) Donald Barry
Captain Fury (United Artists) Brian Aherne
Chip of the Flying U (Universal) Johnny Mack Brown
Code of the Fearless (Spectrum) Tom Tyler
Code of the Secret Service (Warner Bros) Ronald Reagan
Cowboys from Texas (Republic) Robert Livingston
Days of Jesse James (Republic) Roy Rogers
Flying Dueces (RKO) Laurel and Hardy
Frontier Pony Express (Republic) Roy Rogers
Frontiers of '49 (Columbia) William Elliott
Henry Goes Arizona (MGM) Frank Morgan
In Old Caliente (Republic) Roy Rogers
In Old Monterey (Republic) Gene Autry
Juarez (Warner Bros) Paul Muni
Kansas Terrors, The (Republic) Robert Livingston
Law Comes to Texas, The (Columbia) William Elliott
Lone Ranger Rides Again, The (Republic) Robert Livingston
Lone Star Pioneers (Columbia) William Elliott
Man of Conquest (Republic) Richard Dix
Mandrake the Magician (Columbia) Warren Hull
Mountain Rhythm (Republic) Gene Autry
Oklahoma Kid, The (Warner Bros) James Cagney
Racketeers of the Range (RKO) George O'Brien
Real Glory, The (Goldwyn) Gary Cooper
Rough Riders' Round-up (Republic) Roy Rogers
Saga of Death Valley (Columbia) Roy Rogers
Stagecoach (United Artists) John Wayne
Taming of the West, The (Columbia) William Elliott
Texas Wildcats (Victory) Tim McCoy
Thundering West, The (Columbia) Charles Starrett
Trigger Fingers (Victory) Tim McCoy
Wall Street Cowboy (Republic) Roy Rogers
Western Caravans (Columbia) Charles Starrett
Zorro's Fighting Legion (Republic) Reed Hadley

1940

Adventures of Red Ryder (Republic) Don Red Barry
Beyond the Sacramento (Columbia) William Elliott
Billy the Kid in Texas (PRC) Bob Steele
Billy the Kid Outlawed (PRC) Bob Steele
Billy the Kid's Gun Justice (PRC) Bob Steele
Blazing Six Shooters (Columbia) Charles Starrett
Border Legion, The (Republic) Roy Rogers
Bullet Code (RKO) George O'Brien
Bullets for Rustlers (Columbia) Charles Starrett
Carson City Kid (Republic) Roy Rogers
Cherokee Strip (Paramount) Richard Dix
Cheyenne Kid, The (Monogram) Jack Randall
Covered Wagon Days (Republic) Robert Livingston
Deadwood Dick (Columbia) Don Douglas
Drums of Fu Manchu (Republic) Henry Brandon
Drums of the Desert (Monogram) Ralph Byrd
Fargo Kid, The (RKO) Tim Holt
Frontier Crusader (PRC) Tim McCoy
Frontier Vengeance (Republic) Donald Barry
Geronimo (Paramount) Preston Foster
Ghost Valley Raiders (Republic) Donald Barry
Girl From Havana (Republic) Dennis O'Keefe
Grandpa Goes to Town (Republic) James Gleason
Grapes of Wrath, The (20th Century-Fox) Henry Fonda
Gun Code (PRC) Tim McCoy
Haunted Harbor (Republic) Kane Richmond
Heroes of the Saddle (Republic) Robert Livingston
Kit Carson (United Artists) Jon Hall
Law and Order (Universal) Johnny Mack Brown
Light of Western Stars, The (Paramount) Russell Hayden
Lone Star Raiders (Republic) Three Mesquiteers
Lucky Cisco Kid (20th Century-Fox) Cesar Romero
Man from Tumbleweeds, The (Columbia) William Elliott
Mysterious Doctor Satan (Republic) Edward Ciannelli
Oklahoma Renegades (Republic) Robert Livingston
One Man's Law (Republic) Donald Barry
Pioneer Days (Monogram) Jack Randall
Pioneers of the Frontier (Columbia) William Elliott
Pioneers of the West (Republic) Robert Livingston
Pony Post (Universal) Johnny Mack Brown
Prairie Schooners (Columbia) William Elliott

Rancho Grande (Republic) Gene Autry
Range Busters, The (Monogram) Range Busters
Return of Wild Bill, The (Columbia) William Elliott
Riders of Black Mountain (PDC) Tim McCoy
Rocky Mountain Rangers (Republic) Three Mesquiteers
Shooting High (20th Century-Fox) Gene Autry
Terry and the Pirates (Columbia) William Tracy
Texas Stagecoach (Columbia) Charles Starrett
Texas Terrors (Republic) Donald Barry
Trail Blazers, The (Republic) Robert Livingston
Trail of the Vigilantes (Universal) Franchot Tone
Trailing Double Trouble (Monogram) Range Busters
Triple Justice (RKO) George O'Brien
Tulsa Kid, The (Republic) Donald Barry
Under Texas Skies (Republic) Three Mesquiteers
Wagon Train (RKO) Tim Holt
Wagons Westward (Republic) Buck Jones
West of Carson City (Universal) Johnny Mack Brown
When the Daltons Rode (Universal) Randolph Scott
Wildcat of Tucson (Columbia) William Elliott
Young Buffalo Bill (Republic) Roy Rogers

1941
Across The Sierras (Columbia) William Elliott
Adventures of Captain Marvel (Republic) Tom Tyler
Apache Kid, The (Republic) Donald Barry
Arizona Cyclone (Universal) Dick Curtis
Back in the Saddle (Republic) Gene Autry
Bad Man of Deadwood (Republic) Roy Rogers
Bad Men of Missouri (Warner Bros) Dennis Morgan
Bandit Trail, The (RKO) Tim Holt
Belle Starr (20th Century Fox) Randolph Scott
Billy the Kid Wanted (PRC) Bob Steele
Billy the Kid's Fighting Pals (PRC) Bob Steele
Billy the Kid's Range War (PRC) Bob Steele
Boss of Bullion City (Universal) Johnny Mack Brown
Bury Me Not on the Lone Prairie (Universal) Johnny Mack Brown
Death Valley Outlaws (Republic) Donald Barry
Desert Bandit (Republic) Donald Barry
Dick Tracy vs Crime Inc (Republic) Ralph Byrd
Fugitive Valley (Monogram) Range Busters
Gangs of Sonora (Republic) Robert Livingston

Gauchos of El Dorado (Republic) Bob Steele
Go West, Young Lady (Columbia) Glenn Ford
Great Train Robbery, The (Republic) Bob Steele
Hands Across the Rockies (Columbia) William Elliott
Holt of the Secret Service (Columbia) Jack Holt
In Old Cheyenne (Republic) Roy Rogers
Iron Claw, The (Columbia) Charles Quigley
Jesse James at Bay (Republic) Roy Rogers
Jungle Girl (Republic) Frances Gifford
Kansas Cyclone (Republic) Donald Barry
King of Dodge City (Columbia) William Elliott
King of the Texas Rangers (Republic) Sammy Baugh
Law of the Range (Universal) Johnny Mack Brown
Lone Rider Crosses the Rio, The (PRC) George Houston
Lone Rider in Ghost Town, The (PRC) George Houston
Lone Rider Rides On, The (PRC) George Houston
Masked Rider, The (Universal) Johnny Mack Brown
Missouri Outlaw, A (Republic) Donald Barry
Nevada City (Republic) Roy Rogers
North from the Lone Star (Columbia) William Elliott
Outlaws of the Panhandle (Columbia) Charles Starrett
Pals of the Pecos (Republic) Robert Livingston
Phantom Cowboy, The (Republic) Donald Barry
Phantom, The (Columbia) Tom Tyler
Pinto Kid, The (Columbia) Charles Starrett
Prairie Pioneers (Republic) Robert Livingston
Rawhide Rangers (Universal) Johnny Mack Brown
Red River Valley (Republic) Roy Rogers
Return of Daniel Boone, The (Columbia) William Elliott
Riders of Death Valley (Universal) Dick Foran
Riders of the Badlands (Columbia) Charles Starrett
Road Agent (Universal) Dick Foran
Roaring Frontiers (Columbia) William Elliott
Romance of the Rio Grande (20th Century-Fox) Cesar Romero
Saddlemates (Republic) Robert Livingston
Sheriff of Sundown (Republic) Allan Lane
Six-Gun Gold (RKO) Tim Holt
Snake River Desperados (Columbia) Charles Starrett
Son of Davy Crockett, The (Columbia) Bill Elliott
Tarzan's Secret Treasure (MGM) Johnny Weissmuller
They Died With Their Boots On (Warner Bros) Errol Flynn
Thunder Over Prairie (Columbia) Charles Starrett

Two-Gun Sheriff (Republic) Donald Barry
Under Fiesta Stars (Republic) Gene Autry
Underground Rustlers (Monogram) Range Busters
Wanderers of the West (Monogram) Tom Keene
White Eagle (Columbia) Buck Jones
Wyoming Wildcat (Republic) Donald Barry

1942
Along the Sundown Trail (PRC) Art Davis
Arizona Stagecoach (Monogram) Ray Corrigan
Arizona Terrors (Republic) Donald Barry
Bad Men of the Hills (Columbia) Russell Hayden
Billy the Kid Trapped (PRC) Buster Crabbe
Bullets for Bandits (Columbia) William Elliott
Captain Midnight (Columbia) Dave O'Brien
Code of the Outlaw (Republic) Bob Steele
Come On, Danger! (RKO) Tim Holt
Cowboy Serenade (Republic) Gene Autry
Cyclone Kid, The (Republic) Donald Barry
Devil's Trail, The (Columbia) William Elliott
Down Rio Grande Way (Columbia) Charles Starrett
Dudes Are Pretty People (United Artists) Jimmy Rogers
Fighting Bill Fargo (Universal) Johnny Mack Brown
Heart of the Rio Grande (Republic) Gene Autry
Jackass Mail (MGM) Wallace Beery
Jesse James Jr (Republic) Donald Barry
King of the Mounties (Republic) Allan Lane
Lawless Plainsmen (Columbia) Charles Starrett
Lone Rider in Cheyenne, The (PRC) George Houston
Lone Rider in Texas Justice, The (PRC) George Houston
Lone Star Vigilantes (Columbia) William Elliott
Man from Cheyenne (Republic) Roy Rogers
Men of Texas (Universal) Robert Stack
North of the Rockies (Columbia) William Elliott
Omaha Trail, The (MGM) Dean Jagger
Outlaws of Boulder Pass (PRC) George Houston
Outlaws of Pine Ridge (Republic) Donald Barry
Overland Stagecoach (PRC) Robert Livingston
Overland to Deadwood (Columbia) Charles Starrett
Pardon My Gun (Columbia) Charles Starrett
Perils of Nyoka (Republic) Kay Alridge
Perils of the Royal Mounted (Columbia) Robert Stevens

Phantom Plainsmen, The (Republic) Three Mesquiteers
Prairie Gunsmoke (Columbia) William Elliott
Prairie Pals (PRC) Art Davis
Raiders of the Range (Republic) Bob Steele
Raiders of the West (PRC) Bill Rambler Boyd
Ride 'Em Cowboy (Universal) Abbott & Costello
Riders of the Northland (Columbia) Charles Starrett
Riding Through Nevada (Columbia) Charles Starrett
Rolling Down the Great Divide (PRC) Bill Cowboy Boyd
Romance on the Range (Republic) Roy Rogers
Shadows of the Sage (Republic) Bob Steele
Shut My Big Mouth (Columbia) Joe E. Brown
Sombrero Kid, The (Republic) Donald Barry
Sons of the Pioneers (Republic) Roy Rogers
South of Santa Fe (Republic) Roy Rogers
Spy Smasher (Republic) Kane Richmond
Stagecoach Buckaroo (Universal) Johnny Mack Brown
Stagecoach Express (Republic) Donald Barry
Sundown Kid, The (Republic) Donald Barry
Texas Justice (PRC) George Houston
Texas Manhunt (PRC) Lee Powell
Thunder River Feud (Monogram) Range Busters
Thundering Hoofs (RKO) Tim Holt
Tomstone, the Town Too Tough to Die (Paramount) Richard Dix
Tornado in the Saddle, A (Columbia) Russell Hayden
Undercover Man (United Artists) William Boyd
Valley of Hunted Men (Republic) Three Mesquiteers
Valley of Vanishing Men, The (Columbia) Bill Elliott
Vengeance of the West (Columbia) William Elliott
West of Cimarron (Republic) Bob Steele
West of Tombstone (Columbia) Charles Starrett
Westward Ho (Republic) Bob Steele
Wild Bill Hickock Rides (Warner Bros) Bruce Cabot

1943
Avenging Rider, The (RKO) Tim Holt
Batman (Columbia) Lewis Wilson
Beyond the Last Frontier (Republic) Eddie Dew
Black Hills Express (Republic) Donald Barry
Blocked Trail, The (Republic) Bob Steele
Bordertown Gun Fighters (Republic) William Elliott
Bullets and Saddles (Monogram) Ray Corrigan

California Joe (Republic) Donald Barry
Calling Wild Bill Elliott (Republic) William Elliott
Canyon City (Republic) Donald Barry
Captain American (Republic) Dick Purcell
Carson City Cyclone (Republic) Donald Barry
Chatterbox (Republic) Joe E. Brown
Chetniks! The Fighting Guerillas (20th Century Fox) Philip Dorn
Cheyenne Roundup (Universal) Johnny Mack Brown
China (Paramount) Loretta Young
Cowboy in the Clouds (Columbia) Charles Starrett
Daredevils of the West (Republic) Allan Lane
Days of Old Cheyenne (Republic) Donald Barry
Dead Man's Gulch (Republic) Donald Barry
Death Rides the Plains (PRC) Robert Livingston
Death Valley Manhunt (Republic) William Eliott
Devil Riders (PRC) Buster Crabbe
Fighting Buckaroo, The (Columbia) Charles Starrett
Fighting Frontier (RKO) Tim Holt
Fugitive from Sonora (Republic) Donald Barry
Hail to the Rangers (Columbia) Charles Starrett
King of the Cowboys (Republic) Roy Rogers
Law of the Saddle (PRC) Robert Livingston
Man from the Rio Grande, The (Republic) Donald Barry
Man from Thunder River, The (Republic) William Elliott
Outlaws of Santa Fe (Republic) Don Red Barry
Outlaws of Stampede Pass (Monogram) Johnny Mack Brown
Overland Mail Robbery (Republic) William Elliott ·
Ox-Bow Incident, The (20th Century Fox) Henry Fonda
Raiders of Sunset Pass (Republic) Eddie Dew
Rangers Take Over, The (PRC) Dave (Tex O'Brien
Red River Robin Hood (RKO) Tim Holt
Riders of the Rio Grande (Republic) Bob Steele
Santa Fe Scouts (Republic) Bob Steele
Secret Service in Darkest Africa (Republic) Rod Cameron
Silver Spurs (Republic) Roy Rogers
Six-Gun Gospel (Monogram) Johnny Mack Brown
Stranger From Pecos, The (Monogram) Johnny Mack Brown
Tenting Tonight on the Old Camp Ground (Universal) Johnny Mack Brown
Texas Kid, The (Monogram) Johnny Mack Brown
Thundering Trails (Republic) Three Mesquiteers
Wagon Tracks West (Republic) William Elliott
West of Texas (PRC) Texas Rangers

Western Cyclone (PRC) Buster Crabbe
Wild Horse Rustlers (PRC) Robert Livingston
Wolves of the Range (PRC) Robert Livingston

1944
Beneath Western Skies (Republic) Robert Livingston
Big Bonanza, The (Republic) Richard Arlen
Big Noise, The (20th Century Fox) Laurel & Hardy
Black Arrow (Columbia) Mark Roberts
Black Parachute, The (Columbia) John Carradine
Bordertown Trail (Republic) Sunset Carson
Boss of Boomtown (Universal) Rod Cameron
Call of the Rockies (Republic) Sunset Carson
Cheyenne Wildcat (Republic) William Elliott
Code of the Prairie (Republic) Sunset Carson
Cowboy and the Senorita (Republic) Roy Rogers
Drifter, The (PRC) Buster Crabbe
Fighting Seabees, The (Republic) John Wayne
Firebrands of Arizona (Republic) Sunset Carson
Ghost Guns (Monogram) Johnny Mack Brown
Great Alaskan Mystery, The (Universal) Milburn Stone
Hands Across the Border (Republic) Roy Rogers
Hidden Valley Outlaws (Republic) William Elliott
Laramie Trail, The (Republic) Robert Livingston
Law Men (Monogram) Johnny Mack Brown
Lumberjack (United Artists) William Boyd
Marshal of Reno (Republic) William Elliott
Mojave Firebrand (Republic) William Elliott
Mystery Man (United Artists) William Boyd
Old Texas Trail, The (Universal) Rod Cameron
Pride of the Plains (Republic) Robert Livingston
Raiders of Ghost City (Universal) Dennis Moore
San Antonio Kid, The (Republic) William Elliott
San Fernando Valley (Republic) Roy Rogers
Sheriff of Las Vegas (Republic) William Elliott
Silver City Kid (Republic) Allan Lane
Stagecoach to Monterey (Republic) Allan Lane
Sundown Valley (Columbia) Charles Starrett
Trigger Law (Monogram) Hoot Gibson
Trigger Trail (Universal) Rod Cameron
Tucson Raiders (Republic) William Elliott
Vigilantes of Dodge City (Republic) Wild Bill Elliott

Wild Horse Phantom (PRC) Buster Crabbe
Yellow Rose of Texas (Republic) Roy Rogers
Zorro's Black Whip (Republic) Linda Stirling

1945
A Thousand and One Nights (Columbia) Cornel Wilde
Along Came Jones (United Artists) Gary Cooper
Bad Men of the Border (Universal) Kirby Grant
Bandits of the Badlands (Republic) Sunset Carson
Bells of Rosarita, The (Republic) Roy Rogers
Chicago Kid, The (Republic) Donald Barry
China's Little Devils (Monogram) Harry Carey
Code of the Lawless (Universal) Kirby Grant
Colorado Pioneers (Republic) William Elliott
Corpus Christi Bandits (Republic) Allan Lane
Dakota (Republic) John Wayne
Daltons Ride Again, The (Universal) Alan Curtis
Frontier Fugitives (PRC) Texas Rangers
Great Stagecoach Robbery, The (Republic) William Elliott
Gun Smoke (Monogram) Johnny Mack Brown
I'll Be Seeing You (Selznick International) Ginger Rogers
Lawless Empire (Columbia) Charles Starrett
Lone Texas Ranger (Republic) William Elliott
Man from Oklahoma (Republic) Roy Rogers
Manhunt of Mystery Island (Republic) Richard Bailey
Marshal of Laredo (Republic) William Elliott
Oregon Trail (Republic) Sunset Carson
Outlaws of the Rockies (Columbia) Charles Starrett
Phantom of the Plains (Republic) William Elliott
Phantom Rider, The (Republic) Robert Kent
Prairie Rustlers (PRC) Buster Crabbe
Purple Monster Strikes, The (Republic) Dennis Moore
Renegades of the Rio Grande (Universal) Rod Cameron
Rough Riders of Cheyenne (Republic) Sunset Carson
Rough Ridin' Justice (Columbia) Charles Starrett
Rustlers of the Badlands (Columbia) Charles Starrett
Santa Fe Saddlemates (Republic) Sunset Carson
Sheriff of Cimarron (Republic) Sunset Carson
Story of G. I. Joe, The (Cowan Productions) Burgess Meredith
Sunset in El Dorado (Republic) Roy Rogers
Texas Panhandle (Columbia) Charles Starrett
Topeka Terror, The (Republic) Allan Lane

Trail of Kit Carson (Republic) Allan Lane
Under Western Skies (Universal) Martha O'Driscoll
Utah (Republic) Roy Rogers
Wagon Wheels Westward (Republic) William Elliott

1946
Alias Billy the Kid (Republic) Sunset Carson
Beauty and the Bandit (Monogram) Gilbert Roland
California (Paramount) Ray Milland
California Gold Rush (Republic) William Elliott
Caravan Trail, The (PRC) Eddie Dean
Conquest of Cheyenne (Republic) William Elliott
Crimson Ghost, The (Republic) Charles Quigley
Daughter of Don Q (Republic) Kirk Alyn
Days of Buffalo Bill (Republic) Sunset Carson
Desert Horseman, The (Columbia) Charles Starrett
Driftin' River (PRC) Eddie Dean
Drifting Along (Monogram) Johnny Mack Brown
El Paso Kid, The (Republic) Sunset Carson
Fighting Frontiersman, The (Columbia) Charles Starrett
Flying Serpent, The (PRC) George Zucco
Gay Cavalier, The (Monogram) Gilbert Roland
Gun Town (Universal) Kirby Grant
Gunman's Code (Universal) Kirby Grant
Gunning for Vengeance (Columbia) Charles Starrett
Harvey Girls, The (MGM) Judy Garland
Heading West (Columbia) Charles Starrett
Heldorado (Republic) Roy Rogers
Home on the Range (Republic) Monte Hale
In Old Sacramento (Republic) William Elliott
King of the Forest Rangers (Republic) Larry Thompson
Landrush (Columbia) Charles Starrett
Law of the Canyon (Columbia) Charles Starrett
Lawless Breed (Universal) Kirby Grant
Lightning Raiders (PRC)
Lone Prairie, The (Columbia) Russell Hayden
Man From Rainbow Valley, The (Republic) Monte Hale
My Pal Trigger (Republic) Roy Rogers
North of the Border (Screen Guild) Russell Hayden
Out California Way (Republic) Monte Hale
Plainsman and the Lady, The (Republic) William Elliott
Prairie Outlaws (PRC) Eddie Dean

Red River Renegades (Republic) Sunset Carson
Renegades, The (Columbia) Evelyn Keyes
Rio Grande Raiders (Republic) Sunset Carson
Roaring Rangers (Columbia) Charles Starrett
Roll On, Texas Moon (Republic) Roy Rogers
Romance of the West (PRC) Eddie Dean
Rustler's Roundup (Universal) Kirby Grant
Santa Fe Uprising (Republic) Allan Lane
Scarlet Horseman, The (Universal) Paul Guilfoyle
Sheriff of Redwood Valley (Republic) William Elliott
Singin' in the Corn (Columbia) Judy Canova
Six-Gun Man (PRC) Bob Steele
Song of Arizona (Republic) Roy Rogers
South of Monterey (Monogram) Gilbert Roland
Stagecoach to Denver (Republic) Allan Lane
Sun Valley Cyclone (Republic) William Elliott
Terror Trail (Columbia) Charles Starrett
Thunder Town (PRC) Bob Steele
Under Arizona Skies (Monogram) Johnny Mack Brown
Undercover Woman, The (Republic) Stephanie Bachelor
Vacation in Reno (RKO) Jack Haley
Virginian, The (Paramount) Joel McCrea
Wild Beauty (Universal) Don Porter, Dick Curtis
Wild West (PRC) Eddie Dean

1947
Along the Oregon Trail (Republic) Monte Hale
Apache Rose (Republic) Roy Rogers
Bandits of Dark Canyon (Republic) Allan Lane
Belle Starr's Daughter (20th Century-Fox) George Montgomery
Black Hills (Eagle Lion) Eddie Dean
Black Widow, The (Republic) Bruce Edwards
Border Feud (PRC) Lash LaRue
Buffalo Bill Rides Again (Screen Guild) Richard Arlen
Check Your Guns (PRC) Eddie Dean
Cheyenne Takes Over (Eagle-Lion) Lash LaRue
Dead Man's Gold (Screen Guild) Lash LaRue
Fabulous Texan, The (Republic) William Elliott
Fighting Vigilantes, The (Eagle Lion) Lash LaRue
Flashing Guns (Monogram) Johnny Mack Brown
Frontier Revenge (Screen Guild) Lash La Rue
Ghost Town Renegades (PRC) Lash LaRue

Gun Talk (Monogram) Johnny Mack Brown
Homesteaders of Paradise Valley (Republic) Allan Lane
Jack Armstrong (Columbia) John Hart
Jesse James Rides Again (Republic) Clayton Moore
King of the Bandits (Monogram) Gilbert Roland
King of the Wild Horses (Columbia) Preston Foster
Last Frontier Uprising (Republic) Monte Hale
Law of the Lash (PRC) Lash LaRue
Marauders, The (United Artists) William Boyd
Marshal of Cripple Creek (Republic) Allan Lane
Millerson Case, The (Columbia) Warner Baxter
Over the Santa Fe Trail (Columbia) Ken Curtis
Pioneer Justice (PRC) Lash LaRue
Prairie Express (Monogram) Johnny Mack Brown
Raiders of the South (Monogram) Johnny Mack Brown
Range Beyond the Blue (PRC) Eddie Dean
Red Stallion, The (Eagle Lion) Robert Page
Return of the Lash (PRC) Lash LaRue
Ridin' Down the Trail (Monogram) Jimmy Wakely
Robin Hood of Monterey (Monogram) Gilbert Roland
Robin Hood of Texas (Republic) Gene Autry
Rustlers of Devil's Canyon (Republic) Allan Lane
Sea of Grass, The (MGM) Spencer Tracy
Shadow Valley (Eagle Lion) Eddie Dean
Six-Gun Serenade (Monogram) Jimmy Wakely
Slave Girl (Universal) Yvonne De Carlo
Son of Zorro (Republic) George Turner
Stage to Mesa City (PRC) Lash LaRue
Stranger from Ponca City, The (Columbia) Charles Starrett
Trailing Danger (Monogram) Johnny Mack Brown
Under Colorado Skies (Republic) Monte Hale
Vigilante, Fighting Hero of the West (Columbia) Ralph Byrd
Vigilantes of Boomtown (Republic) Allan Lane
Vigilantes Return, The (Universal) Jon Hall
West of Dodge City (Columbia) Charles Starrett
West to Glory (PRC) Eddie Dean
Wild Country (PRC) Eddie Dean
Wild Frontier, The (Republic) Allan Lane
Wistful Widow of Wagon Gap, The (Universal) Abbott & Costello
Wyoming (Republic) William Elliott

1948

Adventures in Silverado (Columbia) William Bishop
Adventures of Frank and Jesse James (Republic) Clayton Moore
Albuquerque (Paramount) Randolph Scott
Black Bart (Universal) Yvonne de Carlo
Black Eagle (Columbia) William Bishop
Blazing Across the Pecos (Columbia) Charles Starrett
Blood on the Moon (RKO) Robert Mitchum
Bold Frontiersman, The (Republic) Allan Lane
California Firebrand (Republic) Monte Hale
Carson City Raiders (Republic) Allan Lane
Congo Bill (Columbia) Don McGuire
Coroner Creek (Columbia) Randolph Scott
Denver Kid, The (Republic) Rocky Lane
Desperadoes of Dodge City (Republic) Allan Lane
Dude Goes West (Allied Artists) Eddie Albert
Far Frontier, The (Republic) Roy Rogers
Gallant Legion, The (Republic) William Eliott
G-Men Never Forget (Republic) Clayton Moore
Grand Canyon Trail (Republic) Roy Rogers
Hawk of Powder River, The (Eagle Lion) Eddie Dean
Homecoming (MGM) Clark Gable
Lightnin' in the Forest (Republic) Donald Barry
Man from Colorado, The (Columbia) Glenn Ford
Mark of the Lash (Screen Guild) Lash LaRue
Marshal of Amarillo (Republic) Allan Lane
Mexican Hayride (Universal) Abbott & Costello
Oklahoma Badlands (Republic) Allan Lane
Old Los Angeles (Republic) William Elliott
Overland Trails (Monogram) Johnny Mack Brown
Phantom Valley (Columbia) Charles Starrett
Plunderers, The (Republic) Rod Cameron
Quick on the Trigger (Columbia) Charles Starrett
Red River (United Artists) John Wayne
Return of the Bad Men (RKO) Randolph Scott
Silver Trails (Monogram) Jimmy Wakely
Son of God's Country (Republic) Monte Hale
Sundown in Santa Fe (Republic) Allan Lane
Superman (Columbia) Kirk Alyn
Timber Trail, The (Republic) Monte Hale
Tornado Range (Eagle Lion) Eddie Dean
Trail to Laredo (Columbia) Charles Starrett

Triggerman (Monogram) Johnny Mack Brown
Untamed Breed (Columbia) Barbara Britton
West of Sonora (Columbia) Charles Starrett
Westward Trail, The (PRC) Eddie Dean

1949
Ambush (MGM) Robert Taylor
Bad Men of Tombstone (Allied Artists) Barry Sullivan
Bandit King of Texas (Republic) Alan Rocky Lane
Bandits of El Dorado (Columbia) Charles Starrett
Batman and Robin (Columbia) Robert Lowery
Blazing Trail, The (Columbia) Charles Starrett
Calamity Jane and Sam Bass (Universal) Yvonne De Carlo
Challenge of the Range (Colubmia) Charles Starrett
Cowboy and the Prizefighter (Eagle Lion) Jim Bannon
Crashing Thru (Monogram) Whip Wilson
Dalton Gang, The (Lippert) Donald Barry
Death Valley Gunfighter (Republic) Allan Lane
Deputy Marshal (Lippert) Jon Hall
Desert Vigilante (Columbia) Charles Starrett
Doolins of Oklahoma, The (Columbia) Randolph Scott
El Paso (Paramount) John Payne
Feathered Serpent, The (Monogram) Roland Winters
Federal Agents vs Underworld Inc (Republic) Kirk Alyn
Fighting Man of the Plains (20th Century-Fox) Randolph Scott
Fighting Redhead, The (Eagle Lion) Jim Bannon
Frontier Investigator (Republic) Allan Lane
Gay Amigo, The (United Artists) Duncan Reynaldo
Ghost of Zorro (Republic) Clayton Moore
Golden Stallion, The (Republic) Roy Rogers
Haunted Trails (Monogram) Whip Wilson
Hellfire (Republic) William Elliott
Home in San Antone (Columbia) Roy Acuff
Horsemen of the Sierras (Columbia) Charles Starrett
I Shot Jesse James (Lippert) John Ireland
King of the Rocket Men (Republic) Tristram Coffin
Laramie (Columbia) Charles Starrett
Last Bandit, The (Republic) William Elliott
Law of the Golden West (Republic) Monte Hale
Loaded Pistols (Columbia) Gene Autry
Massacre River (Allied Artists) Guy Madison
Mysterious Desperado, The (Republic) Tim Holt

Navajo Trail Raiders (Republic) Allan Lane
Outcasts of the Trail (Republic) Monte Hale
Outlaw Country (Screen Guild) Lash LaRue
Pioneer Marshal (Republic) Monte Hale
Powder River Rustlers (Republic) Allan Lane
Prince of the Plains (Republic) Monte Hale
Ranger of Cherokee Strip (Republic) Monte Hale
Red Desert (Lippert) Don Barry
Renegades of the Sage (Columbia) Charles Starrett
Ride, Ryder, Ride (Eagle-Lion) Jim Bannon
Riders in the Sky (Columbia) Gene Autry
Riders of the Dusk (Monogram) Whip Wilson
Rim of the Canyon (Columbia) Gene Autry
Rimfire (Lippert) James Millican
Roll, Thunder, Roll (Eagle Lion) Jim Bannon
San Antone Ambush (Republic) Monte Hale
Sheriff of Wichita (Republic) Allan Lane
Son of Bad Man (Screen Guild) Lash LaRue
Son of Billy the Kid (Screen Guild) Lash LaRue
Sons of New Mexico (Columbia) Gene Autry
South of Death Valley (Columbia) Charles Starrett
South of Rio (Republic) Monte Hale
Square Dance Jubilee (Lippert) Donald Barry
Stampede (Allied Artists) Rod Cameron
State Department: File 649 (Sigmund Neufeld Pictures) William Lundigan
Susanna Pass (Republic) Roy Rogers
Tough Assignment (Lippert) Donald Barry
Valiant Hombre, The (United Artists) Duncan Renaldo
Wyoming Bandit, The (Republic) Allan Lane
Younger Brothers, The (Warner Bros) Wayne Morris

1950
Across the Badlands (Columbia) Charles Starrett
Arizona Cowboy, The (Republic) Rex Allen
Arizona Territory (Monogram) Whip Wilson
Atom Man vs Superman (Columbia) Kirk Alyn
Big Steal, The (RKO) Robert Mitchum
Border Rangers (Lippert) Donald Barry
Broken Arrow (20th Century-Fox) James Stewart
Calamity Jane and the Texan (Columbia) Evelyn Ankers
California Passage (Republic) Forrest Tucker
Cherokee Uprising (Monogram) Whip Wilson

Code of the Silver Sage (Republic) Allan Lane
Colorado Ranger (Lippert) Jimmy Ellison
Colt 45 (Warner Bros) Randolph Scott
Covered Wagon Raid (Republic) Allan Lane
Cow Town (Columbia) Gene Autry
Crooked River (Lippert) Jimmy Ellison
Dallas (Warner Bros) Gary Cooper
Daltons' Women, The (Western Adventures) Lash LaRue
Davy Crockett, Indian Scout (United Artists) George Montgomery
Desperadoes of the West (Republic) Richard Powers
Everybody's Dancin' (Lippert) Donald Barry
Fast on the Draw (Lippert) Jimmy Shamrock Ellison
Fence Riders (Monogram) Whip Wilson
Flying Disc Man From Mars (Republic) Walter Reed
Frisco Tornado (Republic) Allan Lane
Gunfire (Lippert) Donald Barry
Gunmen of Abilene (Republic) Allan Lane
Gunslingers (Monogram) Whip Wilson
Hidden City, The (Monogram) John Sheffield
Hostile Country (Lippert) Jimmy Ellison
I Shot Billy the Kid (Lippert) Donald Barry
Invisible Monster, The (Republic) Richard Webb
James Brothers of Missouri, The (Republic) Keith Richards
Jiggs and Maggie Out West (Monogram) Joe Yule and Renie Riano
Law of the Badlands (RKO) Tim Holt
Law of the Panhandle (Monogram) Johnny Mack Brown
Lightning Guns (Columbia) Charles Starrett
Marshal of Heldorado (Lippert) Jimmie Ellison
Missourians, The (Republic) Monte Hale
Mule Train (Columbia) Gene Autry
Nevadan, The (Columbia) Randolph Scott
Old Frontier, The (Republic) Monte Hale
Outcasts of Black Mesa (Columbia) Charles Starrett
Outlaw Gold (Monogram) Johnny Mack Brown
Outlaws of Texas (Monogram) Whip Wilson
Over the Border (Monogram) Johnny Mack Brown
Pirates of the High Seas (Columbia) Buster Crabbe
Radar Patrol vs Spy King (Republic) Kirk Alyn
Raiders of Tomahawk Creek (Columbia) Charles Starrett
Return of the Frontiersman (Warner Bros) Gordon MacRae
Rio Grande Patrol (RKO Radio) Tim Holt
Rough Riders of Durango (Republic) Allan Lane

Rustlers on Horseback (Republic) Allan Lane
Saddle Tramp (Universal) Joel McCrea
Salt Lake Raiders (Republic) Allan Lane
Savage Horde, The (Republic) William Elliott
Showdown, The (Republic) William Elliott
Silver Raiders (Monogram) Whip Wilson
Stage to Tucson (Columbia) Rod Cameron
Streets of Ghost Town (Columbia) Charles Starrett
Sudden Death (Lippert) Jimmy Ellison, Russ Hayden
Tarzan and the Slave Girl (RKO) Lex Barker
Texan Meets Calamity Jane, The (Columbia) James Ellison
Texas Dynamo (Columbia) Charles Starrett
Tougher They Come, The (Columbia) Wayne Morris
Trail of Robin Hood (Republic) Roy Rogers
Trail of the Rustlers (Columbia) Charles Starrett
Train to Tombstone (Lippert) Donald Barry
Traveling Saleslady, The (Columbia) Joan Davis
Twilight in the Sierras (Republic) Roy Rogers
Vanishing Westerner, The (Republic) Monte Hale
Vigilante Hideout (Republic) Allan Lane
West of the Brazos (Lippert) Jimmy Ellison
West of Wyoming (Monogram) Johnny Mack Brown

1951
Abilene Trail (Monogram) Whip Wilson
Al Jennings of Oklahoma (Columbia) Dan Duryea
Arizona Manhunt (Republic) Michael Chapin
Black Lash, The (Western Adventure) Lash LaRue
Blazing Bullets (Monogram) Johnny Mack Brown
Bonanza Town (Columbia) Charles Starrett
Buckaroo Sheriff of Texas (Republic) Michael Chapin
Callaway Went Thataway (MGM) Fred MacMurray
Cattle Queen (United Artists) Maria Hart
Cave of Outlaws (Universal) Macdonald Carey
Colorado Ambush (Monogram) Johnny Mack Brown
Cyclone Fury (Columbia) Charles Starrett
Dakota Kid, The (Republic) Michael Chapin
Desert of Lost Men (Republic) Allan Lane
Don Daredevil Rides Again (Republic) Ken Curtis
Flaming Feather (Paramount) Sterling Hayden
Fort Dodge Stampede (Republic) Allan Lane
Fort Worth (Warner Bros) Randolph Scott

Gold Raiders (Columbia) Three Stooges
Government Agents vs Phantom Legion (Republic) Walter Reed
Gunplay (RKO) Tim Holt
Hills of Utah, The (Columbia) Gene Autry
Hot Lead (RKO) Tim Holt
I Was an American Spy (Allied Artists) Ann Dvorak
Joe Palooka in Triple Cross (Monogram) Joe Kirkwood
Kid from Amarillo, The (Columbia) Charles Starrett
King of the Bullwhip (Western Adventure) Lash LaRue
Last Outpost, The (Paramount) Ronald Reagan
Lawless Cowboys (Monogram) Whip Wilson
Little Big Horn (Lippert) John Ireland
Longhorn, The (Monogram) William Elliott
Ma and Pa Kettle Back on the Farm (Universal) Marjorie Main
Man From Sonora (Monogram) Johnny Mack Brown
Man in the Saddle, The (Columbia) Randolph Scott
Mask of the Avenger (Columbia) John Derek
Montana Desperado (Monogram) Johnny Mack Brown
Mysterious Island (Columbia) Richard Crane
Nevada Badmen (Monogram) Whip Wilson
New Mexico (United Artists) Lew Ayres
Night Riders of Montana (Republic) Allan Lane
Oklahoma Justice (Monogram) Johnny Mack Brown
Overland Telegraph (RKO) Tim Holt
Pecos River (Columbia) Charles Starrett
Pistol Harvest (RKO) Tim Holt
Prairie Roundup (Columbia) Charles Starrett
Radar Men From the Moon (Republic) George Wallace
Red Mountain (Paramount) Alan Ladd
Redhead and the Cowboy, The (Paramount) Glenn Ford
Ridin' the Outlaw Trail (Columbia) Charles Starrett
Rodeo Queen and the Senorita, The (Republic) Rex Allen
Santa Fe (Columbia) Randolph Scott
Silver Canyon (Republic) Gene Autry
Silver City Bonanza (Republic) Rex Allen
Smoky Canyon (Columbia) Charles Starrett
Spoilers of the Plains (Republic) Roy Rogers
Stage to Blue River (Monogram) Whip Wilson
Stagecoach Driver (Monogram) Whip Wilson
Tarzan's Peril (RKO) Lex Barker
Ten Tall Men (Columbia) Burt Lancaster
Texans Never Cry (Columbia) Gene Autry

Texas Lawmen (Monogram) Johnny Mack Brown
Texas Rangers, The (Columbia) George Montgomery
Thunder in God's Country (Republic) Rex Allen
Thundering Trail, The (Western Adventure) Lash LaRue
Utah Wagon Train (Republic) Rex Allen
Vanishing Outpost, The (Western Adventure) Lash LaRue
Wanted: Dead or Alive (Monogram) Whip Wilson
Wells Fargo Gunmaster (Republic) Allan Lane
Whistling Hills (Monogram) Johnny Mack Brown

1952
African Treasure (Monogram) John Sheffield
Apache War Smoke (MGM) Gilbert Roland
Black Hills Ambush (Republic) Allan Lane
Blackhawk (Columbia) Kirk Alyn
Bomba and the Jungle Girl (Monogram) John Sheffield
Boots Malone (Columbia) William Holden
Border Saddlemates (Republic) Rex Allen
Buffalo Bill in Tomahawk Territory (United Artists) Clayton Moore
Canyon Ambush (Monogram) Johnny Mack Brown
Captain Video, Master of the Stratosphere (Columbia) Judd Holdren
Captive of Billy the Kid (Republic) Allan Lane
Cripple Creek (Columbia) William Bishop
Dead Man's Trail (Monogram) Johnny Mack Brown
Desert Passage (RKO) Tim Holt
Desperadoes' Outpost (Republic) Allan Lane
Duel at Silver Creek (Universal) Audie Murphy
Fargo (Monogram) William Elliott
Frontier Phantom, The (Western Adventure) Lash LaRue
Gunman, The (Monogram) Whip Wilson
Hangman's Knot (Columbia) Randolph Scott
Hawk of Wild River, The (Columbia) Charles Starrett
High Noon (United Artists) Gary Cooper
Indian Uprising (Columbia) George Montgomery
Jungle Drums of Africa (Republic) Clay Moore
Kansas Territory (Monogram) William Elliott
King of the Congo (Columbia) Buster Crabbe
Laramie Mountains (Columbia) Charles Starrett
Last Musketeer, The (Republic) Rex Allen
Leadville Gunslinger (Republic) Allan Lane
Man from the Black Hills (Monogram) Johnny Mack Brown
Maverick, The (Allied Artists) William Elliott

Montana Incident (Monogram) Whip Wilson
Montana Territory (Columbia) Preston Foster
Night Raiders (Monogram) Whip Wilson
Night Stage to Galveston (Columbia) Gene Autry
Old Oklahoma Plains (Republic) Rex Allen
Outlaw Women (Lippert) Marie Windsor
Rancho Notorious (RKO) Marlene Dietrich
Road Agent (RKO) Tim Holt
Son of Geronimo (Columbia) Clayton Moore
Son of Paleface (Paramount) Bob Hope
Springfield Rifle (Warner Bros) Gary Cooper
Target (RKO) Tim Holt
Tarzan's Savage Fury (RKO) Lex Barker
Texas City (Monogram) Johnny Mack Brown
Thundering Caravans (Republic) Rocky Lane
Trail Guide (RKO) Tim Holt
Voodoo Tiger (Columbia) John Weissmuller
Waco (Monogram) William Elliott
Wagon Team (Columbia) Gene Autry
Wild Horse Ambush (Republic) Michael Chapin
Wild Stallion (Monogram) Ben Johnson
Wyoming Roundup (Monogram) Whip Wilson
Zombies of the Stratosphere (Republic) Judd Holdren

1953
Bandits of the West (Republic) Allan Lane
Carson City (Warner Bros) Randolph Scott
Cow Country (Allied Artists) Edmond O'Brien
Down Laredo Way (Republic) Rex Allen
El Paso Stampede (Republic) Allan Lane
Fort Vengeance (Allied Artists) Keith Larsen
Great Adventures of Captain Kidd, The (Columbia) Richard Crane
Gun Belt (United Artists) George Montgomery
Hannah Lee (Realart) John Ireland
Homesteaders, The (Allied Artists) William Elliott
Jack Slade (Allied Artists) Mark Stevens
Kansas Pacific (Allied Artists) Sterling Hayden
Last of the Pony Riders (Columbia) Gene Autry
Lost Planet, The (Columbia) Judd Holdren
Man Behind the Gun, The (Warner Bros) Randolph Scott
Marksman, The (Allied Artists) Wayne Morris
Marshal of Cedar Rock (Republic) Allan Lane

Marshal's Daughter, The (United Artists) Johnny Mack Brown
Pack Train (Columbia) Gene Autry
Rebel City (Allied Artists) William Elliott
Ride Clear of Diablo (Universal) Audie Murphy
Safari Drums (Monogram) John Sheffield
Savage Frontier (Republic) Allan Lane
Son of Belle Starr (Allied Artists) Keith Larsen
Star of Texas (Allied Artists) Wayne Morris
Stranger Wore a Gun, The (Columbia) Randolph Scott
Tall Texan, The (Lippert) Lloyd Bridges
Topeka (Allied Artists) William Elliott
Vigilante Terror (Allied Artists) William Elliott
Winning of the West (Columbia) Gene Autry

1954
Arrow in the Dust (Allied Artists) Sterling Hayden
Battle of Rogue River (Columbia) George Montgomery
Bengal Brigade (Universal) Rock Hudson
Bitter Creek (Allied Artists) William Elliott
Black Dakotas, The (Columbia) Gary Merrill
Bounty Hunter, The (Warner Bros) Randolph Scott
Broken Lance (20th Century-Fox) Spencer Tracy
Cattle Queen of Montana (RKO) Barbara Stanwyck
Desperado, The (Allied Artists) Wayne Morris
Dragonfly Squadron (Allied Artists) John Hodiak
Drum Beat (Warner Bros) Alan Ladd
Drums Across the River (Universal) Audie Murphy
Forty-Niners, The (Allied Artists) William Elliott
Four Guns to the Border (Universal) Rory Calhoun
Hell's Outpost (Republic) Rod Cameron
Khyber Patrol (United Artists) Richard Egan
Killer Leopard (Monogram) John Sheffield
Lawless Rider, The (United Artists) Johnny Carpenter
Lone Gun, The (United Artists) George Montgomery
Man with the Steel Whip (Republic) Richard Simmons
Masterson of Kansas (Columbia) George Montgomery
Outlaw Stallion, The (Columbia) Philip Carey
Overland Pacific (United Artists) Jack Mahoney
Raid, The (20th Century-Fox) Van Heflin
Riding Shotgun (Warner Bros) Randolph Scott
Riding with Buffalo Bill (Columbia) Marshall Reed
They Rode West (Columbia) Robert Francis

Tobor the Great (Republic) Charles Drake
Trader Tom of the China Seas (Republic) Harry Lauter
Two Guns and a Badge (Allied Artists) Wayne Morris
Untamed Heiress (Republic) Judy Canova

1955
Abbott and Costello Meet the Keystone Kops (Universal) Abbott & Costello
Adventures of Captain Africa (Columbia) John Hart
Adventures of Spin and Marty, The (Disney) Tim Considine
Apache Ambush (Columbia) Bill Williams
Apache Woman, The (American Releasing Corp) Joan Taylor
Crashout (Hal E Chester Productions) William Bendix
Five Guns West (American International) John Lund
Gun That Won the West, The (Columbia)
Lay That Rifle Down (Republic) Judy Canova
Man with the Gun (United Artists) Robert Mitchum
Seminole Uprising (Columbia) George Montgomery
Tall Man Riding (Warner Bros) Randolph Scott
Tennessee's Partner (RKO) John Payne
Top Gun (United Artists) Sterling Hayden
Wyoming Renegades (Columbia) Philip Carey

1956
Black Whip, The (Regal) Paul Richards
Blackjack Ketchum, Desperado (Columbia) Howard Duff
Blazing the Overland Trail (Columbia) Lee Roberts
Brass Legend, The (United Artists) Hugh O'Brien
Canyon Raiders (Allied Artists) Whip Wilson
Don't Knock the Rock (Clover Productions) Bill Halen and the Comets
Flesh and the Spur (American International) John Agar
Ghost Town (United Artists) Kent Taylor
I Killed Wild Bill Hickock (Associated Artists) John Forbes
Johnny Concho (United Artists) Frank Sinatra
Lone Ranger, The (Warner Bros) Clayton Moore
Naked Hills, The (Allied Artists) David Wayne
Pardners (Paramount) Martin & Lewis
Secret of Treasure Mountain (Columbia) Raymond Burr
Tension at Table Rock (RKO) Richard Egan
Thunder Over Arizona (Republic) Wallace Ford
White Squaw, The (Columbia) David Brian
Wild Dakotas, The (Associated Film) Bill Williams
World Without End (Allied Artists) Hugh Marlowe

Yaqui Drums (Allied Artists) Rod Cameron

1957
20 Million Miles to Earth (Columbia) William Hopper
Buckskin Lady, The (United Artists) Patricia Medina
Domino Kid, The (Columbia) Rory Calhoun
Duel at Apache Wells (Republic) Anna Maria Alberghetti
Fury at Showdown (United Artists) John Derek
Gun Duel in Durango (United Artists) George Montgomery
Guns of Fort Petticoat, The (Columbia) Audie Murphy
Hell's Crossroads (Republic) Stephen McNally
Iron Sheriff, The (United Artists) Sterling Hayden
Last of the Bad Men (Allied Artists) George Montgomery
Last Stagecoach West (Republic) Jim Davis
Lawless Eighties, The (Republic) Buster Crabbe
Lonely Man, The (Paramount) Jack Palance
Motorcycle Gang (American International) Anne Neyland
Night the World Exploded, The (Columbia) Kathryn Grant
Oklahoman, The (United Artists) Joel McCrea
Outlaw's Son (United Artists) Dane Clark
Phantom Stagecoach, The (Columbia) William Bishop
Sierra Stranger (Columbia) Howard Duff
Storm Rider, The (20th Century-Fox) Scott Brady
Valerie (United Artists) Sterling Hayden
Viking Women and the Sea Serpent (American International) Abby Dalton
War of the Colossal Beast (American International) Sally Fraser

1958
Ambush at Cimarron Pass (20th Century-Fox) Scott Brady
Badman's Country (Warner Bros) George Montgomery
Blood Arrow (20th Century-Fox) Scott Brady
Cole Younger, Gunfighter (Allied Artists) Frank Lovejoy
Escape from Red Rock (20th Century-Fox) Brian Donlevy
From Hell to Texas (20th Century Fox) Don Murray
Gun Fever (United Artists) Mark Stevens
Gunsmoke in Tucson (Allied Artists) Mark Stevens
Man from God's Country (Allied Artists) George Montgomery
Nine Lives of Elfego Baca, The (Buena Vista) Robert Loggia
Old Yeller (Buena Vista) Fess Parker
Plunderers of Painted Flats (Republic) John Carroll
Quantrill's Raiders (Allied Artists) Steve Cochran
Rawhide Trail, The (Allied Artists) Rex Reason

Return to Warbow (Columbia) Philip Carey
Seven Guns to Mesa (Allied Artists) Charles Quinlivan
Teenage Cave Man (American International) Robert Vaughn
Teenage Monster (Marquette Productions) Anne Gwynne
Toughest Gun in Tombstone (United Artists) George Montgomery

1959
30 Foot Bride of Candy Rock, The (Columbia) Lou Costello
Alias Jesse James (United Artists) Bob Hope
Battle of the Coral Sea (Columbia) Cliff Robertson
Cast a Long Shadow (United Artists) Audie Murphy
Escort West (United Artists) Victor Mature
Gunfighters of Abilene (United Artists) Buster Crabbe
Gunmen from Laredo (Columbia) Robert Knapp
Have Rocket Will Travel (Columbia) Three Stooges
Jailbreakers, The (American International) Robert Hutton
Legend of Tom Dooley, The (Columbia) Michael Landon
Lone Texan (20th Century-Fox) Willard Parker
Oregon Trail, The (20th Century-Fox) Fred MacMurray
Thirty-Four Foot Bride of Candy Rock, The (Columbia) Lou Costello

1960
Five Guns to Tombstone (United Artists) James Brown
Noose for a Gunman (United Artists) Jim Davis
Oklahoma Territory (United Artists) Gloria Talbott
One Foot in Hell (20th Century-Fox) Alan Ladd
Plunderers, The (Allied Artists) Jeff Chandler

1961
Gambler Wore a Gun, The (United Artists) Jim Davis

1962
Elfego Baca: Six Gun Law (Buena Vista) Robert Loggia
Panic In Year Zero! (American International) Ray Milland
Three Stooges Meet Hercules, The (Columbia) Three Stooges
Wild Westerners, The (Columbia) James Philbrook

1963
Gunfight at Comanche Creek (Allied Artists) Audie Murphy
Six-Gun Law (Buena Vista) Robert Loggia

1964
Law of the Lawless (Paramount) Dale Robertson
Quick Gun, The (Columbia) Audie Murphy
1965
Black Spurs (Paramount) Rory Calhoun
Harum Scarum (MGM) Elvis Presley
Requiem for a Gunfighter (Embassy) Rod Cameron

1966
Follow Me, Boys! (Buena Vista) Fred MacMurray

1967
Red Tomahawk (Paramount) Howard Keel

1968
Support Your Local Sheriff (United Artists) James Garner

1973
Daring Dobermans, The (Rosamond Productions) Charles Knox Robinson

1978
Deathsport (New World Pictures) David Carradine

1984
Mystic Warrior, The (Warner Bros) Will Sampson

1986
Tomb, The (International Home Video) Cameron Mitchell

1997
Motorcycle Cheerleading Mommas (Timeless Mulimedia) Christopher Mitchum

TELEVISION SHOWS

ADVENTURES OF KIT CARSON, THE (Revue Studios) [August 1951 to November 1955, syndicated, 30 minutes]

Opening sequence for each episode in the series
Bad Man of Briscoe (12-15-51)
Border City (10-18-52)
Border Corsairs (1-12-52)
Broken Spur (12-27-52)
Feud in San Felipe (12-29-51)
Mask of the Vigilantes (1-24-53)
Mojave Desperados (12-6-52)
Outlaw Paradise (9-13-52)
Pledge to Danger (11-15-52)
Singing Wires (11-29-52)
Spoilers of California (12-22-51)
Trap, The (1-5-52)
Trouble in Tuscarora (9-27-52)
Widow of Indian Wells (8-22-53)

ADVENTURES OF RIN TIN TIN (Screen Gems) [October 1954 to May 1959, ABC, 30 minutes]

Ghost Town, The (4-29-55)

ADVENTURES OF WILD BILL HICKOK (Screen Gems) [April 15, 1951 to May 16, 1958, syndicated, CBS 1955-1958, ABC 1957-1958, 30 minutes]

Portions of the opening sequence for each black and white episode
Ambush ()
Battle Line ()
Blake's Kid ()
Ghost Town Lady ()
Halley's Comet ()
Kangaroo Kaper, The ()
Runaway Wizard ()
Silver Stage Holdup ()
Treasure Trail ()

ALIAS SMITH AND JONES (Universal TV) [January 5, 1971 to January 13, 1973, ABC, 60 minutes]

Bushwack! (October 21, 1972)

ANNIE OAKLEY (Flying A Productions) [January 9, 1954 to February 24, 1957, syndicated, 30 minutes]

Portions of the opening sequence for each episode

A Tall Tale (6-17-56)
Annie and the First Phone (7-22-56)
Annie and the Junior Pioneers (3-27-55)
Annie and the Lacemaker (7-15-56)
Annie and the Leprechauns (9-2-56)
Annie and the Six o'Spades (7-31-54)
Annie Finds Strange Treasure (3-6-54)
Annie Helps a Drifter (6-6-54)
Annie Joins the Calvalry (5-22-54)
Annie's Desert Adventure (4-24-54)
Diablo Doctor (3-13-55)
Dilemma at Diablo (9-9-56)
Front Trail, The (11-11-56)
Grubstake Bank (12-16-56)
Indian Justice (7-29-56)
Joker on Horseback (6-10-56)
Justice Guns (4-17-54)
Mississippi Kid, The (8-12-56)
Renegade's Return (8-19-56)
Robin Hood Kid, The (7-1-56)
Runaways, The (7-24-54)
Saga of Clement O'Toole, The (11-4-56)
Shadow at Sonoma (9-23-56)
Sugarfoot Sue (8-26-56)
Sure Shot Annie (4-17-55)
Thunder Hill (4-10-55)
Tomboy, The (7-17-54)
Tuffy (2-3-57)
Valley of the Shadows (3-20-54)

BAT MASTERSON (ZIV Television Productions) [October 8, 1958 to June 1, 1961, NBC, 30 minutes]

A Personal Matter (1-28-59)
Bat Trap (10-13-60)
Buffalo Kill (7-29-59)
Bullwhacker's Bounty (2-16-61)
Cattle and Canes (3-3-60)
Dynamite Blows Two Ways (10-22-58)
End of the Line (1-26-61)
Flume to the Mother Lode (1-28-60)
Last of the Night Raiders (11-24-60)
Pigeon and Hawk (1-21-60)
Snare, The (3-17-60)

BIG VALLEY, THE (Four Star Television) [September 15, 1965 to May 19, 1969, ABC, 60 minutes)

A Stranger Everywhere (12-9-68)

BLACK SADDLE (Four Star Television) [January 10, 1959 to May 6, 1960, NBC, 30 minutes]

Client: Braun (4-4-59)

BONANZA (NBC) [September 12, 1959 to January 16, 1973, NBC, 60 minutes]

A Knight to Remember (12-20-64)
Auld Sod, The (2-4-62)
Beginning, The (11-25-62)
Blood Line, The (12-31-60)
Boss, The (5-19-63)
Breed of Violence (11-5-60)
Caution, Easter Bunny Crossing (3-29-70)
Crucible, The (4-8-62)
Cutthroat Junction (3-18-61)
Day of Reckoning (10-22-60)
Day of the Dragon (12-3-61)
Deadly Ones, The (12-2-62)
Death on Sun Mountain (9-19-59)
Denver McKee (10-15-60)
Desert Justice (2-20-60)
Dowry, The (4-29-62)
Escape to Ponderosa (3-5-60)
Far, Far Better Thing, The (1-10-65)
Frenchman, The (12-10-61)
Gamble, The (4-1-62)
Hayburner, The (2-17-63)
Honor of Cochise (10-8-61)
Invention of a Gunfighter (9-20-64)
King of the Mountain (2-23-64)
Last Trophy, The (3-26-60)
Last Viking, The (11-12-60)
Long Night, The (5-6-62)
Look to the Stars (3-18-62)
Meena (11-16-69)
My Brother's Keeper (4-7-63)
Paiute War, The (10-3-59)
Passing of a King, The (10-13-68)
Rescue, The (2-25-61)
Ride, The (1-21-62)
Savage, The (12-3-60)
Scapegoat, The (10-25-64)

Secret, The (5-6-61)
Smiler, The (9-24-61)
Spitfire, The (1-14-61)
Strange One, The (11-14-65)
Underdog, The (12-13-64)
Unwanted, The (4-6-69)
Vengeance (2-11-61)
Walter and the Outlaws (5-24-64)
War Comes to Washoe, The (11-4-62)
Way of Aaron, The (3-10-63)

BRANDED (Goodson-Todman Productions) [January 24, 1965 to September 4, 1966, NBC, 30 minutes]

Vindicators, The (1-31-65)

BRAVE EAGLE (NBC) [September 28, 1955 to March 14, 1956, CBS, 30 minutes]

Blood Brother (9-28-55)
Challenge, The (12-21-55)
Code of a Chief (11-23-55)
Cry of the Heron (10-5-55)
Face of Fear (11-30-55)
Flight, The (11-16-55)
Gold of Haunted Mountain (10-19-55)
Mask of Manitou (11-9-55)
Moonfire (11-2-55)
Search for the Sun (10-26-55)
Shield of Honor (12-14-55)
Treachery of At-Ta-Tu, The (10-12-55)
Voice of the Serpent (12-7-55)
Witch Bear (3-7-56)

BROKEN ARROW (TCF Television Productions) [September 25, 1956 to June 24, 1958, ABC, 30 minutes]

Return From the Shadows (12-4-56)

BUFFALO BILL JR (Flying A Productions) [March 1, 1955 to September 21, 1956, syndicated, 30 minutes]

Opening sequence for each episode
Apache Raid (7-27-55)
Boomer's Blunder (4-1-55)
Calico Kid, The (5-15-55)
Death of Johnny Ringo, The (3-22-55)
Fight For Texas (7-27-55)
Grave of the Monsters (5-24-55)

Pawnee Stampede (5-19-55)
Rails Westward (7-30-55)
Red Hawk (5-28-55)
Runaway Renegade (3-1-55)
Trail of the Killer (3-4-55)

CADE'S COUNTY (20th Century-Fox Television) [September 19, 1971 to April 9, 1972, CBS, 60 minutes]

Mustangers, The (11-14-71)

CALIFORNIANS, THE (California Film Enterprises) [September 24, 1957 to May 26, 1959, NBC, 30 minutes]

Long Night, The (12-23-58)

CAPTAIN Z-RO (W. A. Palmer Films) [November 1951 to June 10, 1956, syndicated, 30 minutes]

Pony Express (1-28-56)

CIMARRON STRIP (CBS) [September 7, 1967 to March 7, 1968, CBS, 90 minutes]

Big Jessie (2-8-68)
Fool's Gold (1-11-68)

CIRCUS BOY (Screen Gems) [September 23, 1956 to December 12, 1957, NBC for season 1, ABC for season 2, 30 minutes]

Masked Marvel, The (12-9-56)

CISCO KID, THE (ZIV Television) [September 5, 1950 to March 22, 1956, syndicated, 30 minutes]

Battle of Red Rock Pass (11-5-53)
Dog Story (12-26-50)
Ghost Story (10-15-51)
Ghost Town (2-12-52)
Hidden Valley (12-11-51)
Jewelry Holdup (2-5-52)
Quarter Horse (1-29-52)
Quicksilver Murder (2-12-52)
Spanish Dagger (2-19-52)
Stolen Bonds (9-10-51)
Vigilante Story (12-4-51)
Water Rights (2-20-51)

COWBOY G-MEN (Telemount-Mutual Productions) [September 13, 1952 to June 13, 1953, syndicated, 30 minutes]

Chinaman's Chance (9-20-52)
Bounty Jumpers (11-22-52)
Koniackers (12-6-52)
Salted Mines (12-20-52)
Hang the Jury (1-17-53)
Silver Fraud (3-14-53)
Empty Mailbags (4-11-53)
Sawdust Swindle (4-18-53)
Sidewinder, The (5-2-53)

DEATH VALLEY DAYS (Pacific Coast Borax Company) [March 1, 1952 to April 24, 1970, syndicated, 30 minutes]

Deserters, The (11-6-60)
Journey, The (3-29-65)

DUSTY'S TRAIL (Metromedia Producers) [September 11, 1973 to March 12, 1974, syndicated, 30 minutes]

Portions of the opening sequence of each episode
Tomahawk Terriroty (10-30-73)

FAMILY THEATER (St. Paul Films) [1951 to 1958, syndicated, 60 minutes]

Hill Number One (3-25-51)

FRONTIER DOCTOR (Hollywood Television Service) [September 26, 1958 to June 20, 1959, ABC, 30 minutes]

Opening sequence to each episode
A Twisted Road (4-25-59)
Crooked Circle (10-18-58)
Drifting Sands (3-28-59)
Fury of the Big Top (11-22-58)
Gringo Pete (5-2-59)
The Outlaw Legion (11-15-58)

FUGITIVE, THE (Quinn Martin Productions) [September 17, 1963 to August 29, 1967, ABC, 60 minutes]

Nicest Fella You'd Ever Want to Meet (1-19-65)
Shattered Silence, The (4-11-67)

FURY (Television Programs of America) [October 15, 1955 to March 19, 1960, NBC, 30 minutes]

Portions of the Opening Sequence of each episode
4-H Story, The (12-17-55)
Baby, The (4-7-56)
Choice, The (2-4-56)
Fury Runs to Win (3-10-56)
Ghost Town (12-31-55)
Hobo, The (1-7-56)
Horse Coper, The (10-29-55)
Joey and the Gypsies (11-26-55)
Joey Saves the Day (12-10-55)
Joey Sees It Through (1-21-56)
Joey's Dame Trouble (11-19-55)
Joey's Father (12-3-55)
Junior Rodeo (12-24-55)
Miracle, The (2-25-56)
Scorched Earth (11-12-55) [end of episode was first appearance of the Fury
    Ranch Set]
Stolen Fury (1-28-56)
Test, The (3-3-56)
Trial by Jury (10-27-56)

GENE AUTRY SHOW, THE (Flying A Productions) [July 23, 1950 to August 7, 1956, CBS, 30 minutes]

Bandits of Boulder Bluff, The (11-24-51)
Battle Axe (8-31-54)
Feuding Friends (11-26-55)
Guns Below the Border (11-5-55)
Law Comes to Scorpion (10-22-55)
Rio Renegades (9-29-53)
Stage to San Dimas, The (10-8-55)
Warning Danger (11-10-51)

GUNSMOKE (Filmaster Productions) [September 10, 1955 to March 31, 1975, CBS, 30 minutes (1st 6 seasons)/60 minutes]

Claustrophobia (1-25-58)
Killer at Large (2-5-66)
Legal Revenge (11-17-56)
Outlaw's Woman (12-11-65)
Photographer, The (4-6-57)

HAVE GUN WILL TRAVEL (CBS Productions) [September 14, 1957 to April 20, 1963, CBS, 30 minutes]

A Snare for Murder (11-22-58)
Ballad of Oscar Wilde, The (12-6-58)
Chase, The (4-11-59)

Fatalist, The (9-10-60)
Fight At Adobe Wells (3-12-60)
Gold and Brimstone (6-20-59)
Genesis (9-15-62)
Heritage of Anger (6-6-59)
High Wire (11-2-57)
Jenny (1-23-60)
Juliet (1-31-59)
Lady, The (11-15-58)
Long Night, The (11-16-57)
Love of a Bad Woman (3-26-60)
Misguided Father, The (2-27-60)
Monster of Moon Ridge, The (2-28-59)
O'Hare Story, The (3-1-58)
Prophet, The (1-2-60)
Ransom (6-4-60)
Return of the Lady, The (2-21-59)
Show of Force (11-9-57)
Sons of Aaron Murdock, The (5-9-59)
Strange Vendetta (10-26-57)
Three Bells to Perdido (9-14-57)
Trial, The (6-11-60)
Twins, The (5-21-60)
Young Gun (11-8-58)
Yuma Treasure, The (12-14-57)

HIGHWAY PATROL (ZIV Television Programs) [October 5, 1955 to 1959 , syndicated, 30 minutes]

Plane Crash (season 1, episode 23)

HOPALONG CASSIDY (B. B. Productions) [June 24, 1949 to 1952, NBC, 30 minutes]

Alien Range (10-1-52)
Ghost Trails (10-28-52)
Lawless Legacy, The (12-31-52)
Marked Cards (10-28-52)
Vanishing Herd, The (12-12-52)

JOHNNY RINGO (Four Star Productions) [October 2, 1959 to June 30, 1960, CBS, 30 minutes]

Arrival, The (10-2-59)
Cat, The (12-3-59)
Dead Wait (11-19-59)
Rafferty's, The (2-25-60)

LARAMIE (Revue Studios) [September 15, 1959 to May 21, 1963, NBC, 60 minutes]

Saddle and Spur (3-29-60)

LIFE AND LEGEND OF WYATT EARP, THE (Desilu) [September 6, 1955 to June 27, 1961, ABC, 30 minutes]

A Papa For Butch and Ginger (5-9-61)
Apache Gold (3-7-61)
Bat Jumps the Reservation (2-10-59)
Behan's Double Game (3-29-60)
Command Performance (2-19-57)
Convict's Revenge, The (4-4-61)
Doctor, The (10-4-60)
Dodge City Gets a New Marshal (9-4-56)
Dodge City—Hail and Farewell (9-1-59)
Don't Get Tough With the Sailor (2-23-60)
Dull Knife Strikes For Freedom (5-7-57)
Fanatic, The (11-22-60)
Frontier Surgeon (1-19-60)
Gatling Gun, The (10-21-58)
Get Shotgun Gibbs (12-22-59)
His Life in His Hands (3-22-60)
Horse Thief (1-10-61)
How to be a Sheriff (3-24-59)
John Clum, Fighting Editor (4-12-60)
Johnny Behan Falls in Love (2-14-61)
Johnny Ringo's Girl (12-13-60)
Just Before the Battle (6-13-61
Justice (12-25-56)
Last Stand at Smoky Hill (1-20-59)
Lineup for Battle (9-29-59)
Little Gray Home in the West (5-12-59)
Nugget and the Epitaph, The (10-6-59)
Paymaster, The (12-1-59)
Requiem for Old Man Clanton (5-30-61)
Scout, The (3-1-60)
Shoot to Kill (10-18-60)
Siege at Little Alamo (2-5-57)
Study of a Crooked Sheriff (10-25-60)
Three (5-13-58)
Time For All Good Men, The (6-4-57)
Trail to Tombstone, The (9-8-59)
Truth About Old Man Clanton (9-27-60)
Truth About Rawhide Geraghty, The (2-17-59)
Wells Fargo Calling Marshal Earp (12-29-59)
Wyatt Takes the Primrose Path (3-28-61)

Wyatt Wins One (11-10-59)
Wyatt's Brothers Join Up (6-6-61)
You Can't Fight City Hall (10-20-59)

LONE RANGER, THE (Ajax Film/Wrather Productions) [September 15, 1949 to June 6, 1957, ABC, 30 minutes]

Opening and Ending of each episode
A Harp for Hannah (1-31-57)
A Message from Abe (2-7-57)
Angel and the Outlaw (5-23-57)
Avenger, The (1-10-57)
Banker's Son, The (5-16-57)
Barnaby Boggs, Esquire (2-2-50)
Black Hat, The (5-18-50)
Blind Witness (5-30-57)
Breaking Point, The (1-24-57)
Buried Treasure (3-2-50)
Cannonball McKay (12-29-49)
Canuck (4-25-57)
Clover in the Dust (3-7-57)
Courage of Tonto (1-17-57)
Dead-Eye (2-28-57)
Decision for Chris McKeever (12-6-56)
Devil's Pass (5-25-50)
Enter The Lone Ranger (9-15-49)
Finders Keepers (12-8-49)
Ghost Town Fury (3-28-57)
Jim Tyler's Past (2-16-50)
Journey to San Carlos (5-9-57)
Law and Miss Aggie, The (4-11-57)
Legion of Old-Timers (10-6-49)
Letter Bride, The (11-15-56)
Lone Ranger Fights On (9-22-49)
Lone Ranger Triumphs, The (9-29-49)
Man With Two Faces, The (2-23-50)
Masked Rider, The (12-15-49)
No Handicap (10-4-56)
Old Joe's Sister (12-22-49)
Outlaw Masquerade (1-3-57)
Outlaws in Grease Paint (6-6-57)
Outlaw of the Plains (7-6-50)
Prince of Buffalo Gap (4-4-57)
Return of Don Pedro O'Sullivan, The (10-25-56)
Return of the Convict, The (12-1-49)
Rustler's Hideout (10-13-49)
Sheep Thieves (2-9-50)
Sheriff of Smoke Tree, The (9-20-56)

Six Gun's Legacy (11-24-49)
Tarnished Star, The (4-18-57)
Trouble at Tylerville (12-13-56)
Troubled Waters (3-9-50)
Turning Point, The (2-21-57)
Two Against Two (3-21-57)
War Horse (10-20-49)
Whimsical Bandit, The (8-31-50)

MACKENZIE'S RAIDERS (ZIV Television Programs) [October 1, 1958 to 1959, syndicated, 30 minutes]

Long Day, The (10-17-58)
Death by the Numbers (10-24-58)
Deadly Mirror (11-7-58)
Renegade, The (12-5-58)
Dream of Empire (12-13-58)
Thunder Stick (1-31-59)
Scalp Hunters, The (2-28-59)
Pen and the Sword, The (3-14-59)
Poisoners, The (3-21-59)
Mutiny (4-11-59)
Joe Ironhat (4-25-59)
Uprising (5-9-59)
Lucinda Cabot (5-30-59)
Missing—Presumed Dead (6-6-59)
Ambush (6-20-59)

OUTLAWS (NBC) [September 29, 1960 to May 10, 1962, NBC, 60 minutes]

Thirty a Month (9-2-60)

OVERLAND TRAIL (Revue Studios) [February 7, 1960 to July 2, 1960, NBC, 60 minutes]

O'Mara's Ladies, The (2-14-60)
Westbound Stage (3-6-60)

PERRY MASON (Paisano Productions) [September 21, 1957 to May 22, 1966, CBS, 60 minutes]

Case of the Ancient Romero, The (5-5-62)
Case of the Bashful Burro, The (3-26-60)
Case of the Bouncing Boomerang, The (12-12-63)
Case of the Counterfeit Crank, The (4-28-62)
Case of the Hasty Honeymooner, The (10-24-65)

PONY EXPRESS (California National Productions) [1959 to May 31, 1960, syndicated, 30 minuts]

Portions of the introduction to each episode
Good Samaritan, The (11-11-59)
Wrong Rope, The (5-17-60)

RANGE RIDER, THE (Flying A Productions) [April 5, 1951 to September 1, 1953, syndicated, 30 minutes]

Blind Trail, The (2-22-53)
Buckskin, The (5-21-53)
Chase, The (1953)
Outlaw Pistols (8-25-53)

REAL McCOYS, THE (Brennan-Westgate Marterto Productions) [October 3, 1957 to June 23, 1963, ABC for 5 years, CBS for 1 year, 30 minutes]

Californy, Here We Come (Pilot Episode) (10-3-57)

RESTLESS GUN, THE (Revue Studios) [September 23, 1957 to June 22, 1959, NBC, 30 minutes]

Code for a Killer (4-27-59)
Duel at Lockwood (9-23-57)

RIFLEMAN, THE (Four Star Television) [September 30, 1958 to April 8, 1963, ABC, 30 minutes]

Conflict (12-24-62)
Deadeye Kid, The (2-10-59)
Executioner, The (5-7-62)
First Wages (10-9-61)
Skull (1-1-62)
Spiked Rifle, The (11-24-59)

RODEO ROUNDUP (KNBH) [May 30, 1953 to July 18, 1953, syndicated, 60 minutes]

Weekly hour-long television show which aired on KNBH channel 4 in Los Angeles at 4:30 pm in 1953 (and syndicated) on the following dates:

5-30
6-6, featured Miss Edie Moore
6-13
6-20, included a wedding
6-27
7-4

7-11
7-18

ROUGH RIDERS, THE (ZIV Television Programs) [October 2, 1958 to September 24, 1959, ABC, 30 minutes]

Ransom of Rita Renee (6-11-59)

ROUTE 66 (Screen Gems) [October 7, 1960 to March 20, 1964, CBS, 60 minutes]

Journey to Nineveh (9-28-62)

ROY ROGERS SHOW, THE (Roy Rogers Productions) [December 30, 1951 to June 9, 1957, NBC, 30 minutes]

Portions of the opening sequence to each episode
Ambush (1-15-56)
And Sudden Death (10-9-55)
Backfire (10-10-54)
Bad Company (12-27-53)
Bad Neighbors (11-21-54)
Badman's Brother (2-10-52)
Big Chance, The (1-23-55)
Blind Justice (12-14-52)
Born Fugitive (2-27-55)
Boys' Day in Paradise Valley (11-7-54)
Brady's Bonanza (3-31-57)
Carnival Killer (6-8-52)
Dead Men's Hill (3-15-52)
Death Medicine (9-7-52)
Doc Stevens' Traveling Store (1-6-52)
Doublecrosser, The (6-1-1952)
End of the Trail (1-27-57)
Fighting Sire (12-16-56)
Flying Bullets (6-15-52)
Ghost Gulch (3-30-52)
Ghost Town Gold (5-25-52)
Go For Your Guns (11-23-52)
Gun Trouble (11-22-53)
Hard Luck Story (10-31-54)
Hidden Treasures (12-19-54)
Hijackers, The (10-24-54)
His Weight in Wildcats (11-11-56)
Horse Crazy (2-26-56)
Junior Outlaw (2-10-57)
Knockout, The (12-28-52)
Lady Killer, The (9-12-54)
Land Swindle, The (3-14-54)

Last of the Larabee Kid (10-17-54)
Loaded Guns (4-12-53)
Long Chance, The (5-24-53)
M Stands For Murder (12-6-53)
Mayor of Ghost Town, The (11-30-52)
Milliner from Medicine Creek (10-11-53)
Mingo Kid, The (4-26-53)
Money is Dangerous (1-29-56)
Money to Burn (6-28-53)
Morse Mix Up, The (3-24-56)
Outlaw's Girl (2-17-52)
Outlaws of Paradise Valley (11-8-53)
Outlaw's Return (9-28-52)
Outlaws' Town (3-1-52)
Pat's Inheritance (11-1-53)
Peddler From Pecos, The (12-13-53)
Shoot to Kill (4-27-52)
Phantom Rustlers (4-5-53)
Ranch War (10-23-55)
Ride in the Death Wagon (4-6-52)
Ride of the Ranchers, The (4-20-52)
Run-A-Round, The (2-22-53)
Scavenger, The (11-27-55)
Secret of Indian Gap, The (1-24-54)
Set-Up, The (1-20-52)
Sheriff Missing (3-17-56)
Shoot to Kill (4-27-52)
Strangers (12-5-54)
Tossup (12-2-56)
Train Robbery, The (2-3-52)
Treasure of Howling Dog Canyon, The (1-27-52)
Unwilling Outlaw, The (3-8-52)
Violence in Paradise Valley (11-2-55)

SKY KING (Jack Chertok Television) [September 16, 1951 to March 8, 1959, NBC (9-16-51 to 10-26-52), ABC (11-8-52 to 9-54), syndicated (1955 to 1959), 30 minutes]

Wild Man, The (12-28-58)

STAGECOACH WEST (Four Star Productions) [October 4, 1960 to June 27, 1961, ABC, 60 minutes]

Finn McColl (1-24-61)

STEVE DONOVAN WESTERN MARSHAL (Vibar TV Film Production) [September 24, 1955 to June 16, 1956, syndicated, 30 minutes]

Portions of the opening sequence to each episode
Comanche Kid (1-14-56)
Napoleon's Eagle (12-17-55)

STORIES OF THE CENTURY (Hollywood Television Service) [January 23, 1954 to March 11, 1955, syndicated, 30 minutes]

Apache Kid (1-9-55)
Augustine Chacon (1-30-55)
Bill Longley (5-20-54)
Billy the Kid (1-30-54)
Black Bart (5-6-54)
Black Jack Ketchum (6-24-54)
Burt Alvord (1-2-55)
Cattle Kate (2-28-54)
Cherokee Bill (2-1-55)
Dalton Gang, The (3-18-54)
Doc Holiday (3-25-54)
Frank and Jesse James (2-7-54)
Henry Plummer (5-13-54)
Joaquin Murietta (4-16-54)
John Wesley Hardin (4-9-54)
Kate Bender (1-23-55)
L. H. Musgrove (3-11-55)
Little Britches (6-17-54)
Milt Sharp (2-28-55)
Quantrill and His Raiders (2-21-54)
Tom Bell (1-16-55)

SUPERMAN (Superman Inc) [September 19, 1952 to April 28, 1958, ABC, 30 minutes]

Big Squeeze, The (9-25-53)
Five Minutes to Doom (9-25-53)
Man Who Could Read Minds, The (10-3-53)

TALES OF THE TEXAS RANGERS (Screen Gems) [August 27, 1955 to December 26, 1958, CBS, 30 minutes])

Carnival Crisscross (9-3-55)

TALES OF WELLS FARGO (Revue Studios) [March 18, 1957 to June 2, 1962, NBC, 30 minutes (seasons 1 through 5), 60 minutes (season 6)]

Portions of the Opening and Ending Sequences for each episode except season 6
Alder Gulch (4-8-57)
Alias Jim Hardie (3-10-58)

Bill Longley (2-10-58)
Billy the Kid (j10-21-57)
Dr. Alice (2-23-58)
Gun, The (4-14-58)
Hank (11-4-57)
Hijackers, The (6-17-57)
Newspaper, The (3-24-58)
Prisoner, The (2-17-58)
Renegade, The (5-12-58)
Shotgun Messengers (5-7-57)
Special Delivery (3-31-58)
Stage West (1-13-58)
Target, The (10-7-57)
Thin Rope, The (3-18-57)
Two Cartridges (9-16-57)
Witness, The (12-30-57)

TEXAN, THE (Desilu) [September 29, 1958 to September 5, 1960, CBS, 30 minutes]

A Time of the Year (12-22-58)
Blue Norther (10-12-59)
Cowards Don't Die (11-30-59)
Easterner, The (12-15-58)
First Notch, The (10-20-58)
Governor's Lady, The (3-14-60)
Image of Guilt (9-21-59)
Johnny Tuvo (5-30-60)
Lady Tenderfoot (5-9-60)
Letter of the Law (3-23-59)
Man Behind the Star, The (2-9-59)
Man Hater, The (6-15-59)
No Way Out (9-14-59)
Outpost (1-19-59)
Return to Friendly (2-2-59)
Showdown at Abilene (11-9-59)
South of the Border (5-18-59)
Stampede (11-2-59)
Taming of Rio Nada, The (1-11-60)
Telegraph Story, The (10-26-59)
Terrified Town, The (1-25-60)
Trouble on the Trail (11-23-59)

T.H.E. CAT (NBC Productions) [September 16, 1966 to March 31, 1967, NBC, 30 minutes]

One episode, possibly "A Hot Place to Die" (1-13-67)

TOMBSTONE TERRITORY (ZIV Television Programs) [October 16, 1957 to 1960, ABC for 2 years, then syndicated, 30 minutes]

Gun Hostage (5-1-59)
Innocent Man, The (5-13-60)

TRACKDOWN (Four Star Television) [October 4, 1957 to September 23, 1959, CBS, 30 minutes]

Reward, The (1-3-58)

UNION PACIFIC (California National Productions) [April 1958 to September 1959, syndicated, 30 minutes]

Black Hills Incident (9-27-58)
Bridge at Devil's Canyon (11-15-58)
Bullock Incident (4-4-59)
Cave-In (l6-6-59)
Challenge, The (10-25-58)
Challenger, The (12-20-58)
Charming Rustler, The (3-7-59)
Cheyenne Incident, The (4-11-59)
Choice, The (3-28-59)
Counterfeit Lady (3-14-59)
Dale Incident, The (12-6-58)
Deadline (10-4-58)
DeKett Territory (11-22-58)
End of Track (11-29-58)
Glass Bullet, The (5-30-59)
Haunted Hills, The (12-13-58)
Impractical Joker, The (12-27-58)
Indian Treaty (11-8-58)
Lost Boy (2-28-59)
Medicine Show (1958)
Nineteen to Cheyenne (2-21-59)
Patterns for Revenge (1-17-59)
Pawnee Bill (2-14-59)
Payroll to Cheyenne (10-18-58)
Prison Camp (2-7-59)
Railroad Doctor (1-31-59)
Ring of Iron (5-23-59)
Roadblock (1-10-59)
Runaway (4-18-59)
Supply Train (3-21-59)
Surveyor, The (11-1-58)
Ten to a Rail (5-16-59)
To the Death (l6-13-59)
Trestle, The (5-2-59)

Wedding, The (4-25-59)
Women with Guns (5-9-59)
Yesterday's Killer (10-11-58)

VIRGINIAN, THE (Revue Studios) [September 19, 1962 to March 24, 1971 NBC, 90 minutes]

Mountain of the Sun, The (4-17-63)
Run Quiet (11-13-63)
Strangers at Sundown (4-3-63)

WAGON TRAIN (Revue Studios) [September 18, 1957 to May 2, 1965, NBC, 60 minutes]

Stagecoach Story, The (9-30-59)
Tent City Story, The (12-10-58)

WALT DISNEY WONDERFUL WORLD OF COLOR (Walt Disney Productions) [October 2, 1957 to March 12, 1958, 6 episodes, ABC, 60 minutes)

Saga of Andy Burnett, The

WANTED DEAD OR ALIVE (Four Star Television) [September 6, 1958 to March 29, 1961, CBS, 30 minutes]

Bad Gun (10-24-59)
Dead End (9-27-58)
Dead Reckoning (3-22-61)
Desert Seed (11-14-59)
Die by the Gun (12-6-58)
Drop to Drink (12-27-58)
Eager Man (2-28-59)
Epitaph (2-8-61)
Estralita (10-3-59)
Favor, The (11-15-58)
Journey for Josh (10-5-60)
Monday Morning (3-8-61)
Passing of Shawnee Bill (10-4-58)
Sheriff of Red Rock (11-29-58)
Twelve Hours to Crazy Horse (11-21-59)

WHISPERING SMITH (Revue Studios) [May 8, 1961 to October 30, 1961, NBC, 60 minutes]

Blind One, The (5-8-61)

WRANGLER, THE (NBC) [August 4, 1960 to September 15, 1960, NBC, 30 minutes]

Affair with Browning's Woman, The (8-25-60)

ZANE GREY THEATER (Four Star Productions) [October 5, 1956 to May 18, 1961, CBS, 30 minutes]

Decision at Wilson's Creek (5-17-57)
Hand On the Latch (10-29-59)
Hanging Fever (3-12-59)
Killer Instinct (3-17-60)
Law and the Gun, The (6-4-59)
Man From Everywhere (4-13-61)
Vengeance Canyon (11-30-56)

ZORRO (Walt Disney Productions) [October 10, 1957 to July 2, 1959 ABC, 30 minutes]

Horse of Another Color (10-23-58)
Zorro Rides to the Mission (10-24-57)

RENTAL FILMS

LIVING BIBLE, THE (Family Films) [1952-1953, syndicated, 15-20 minutes]

Birth of the Savior
Childhood of Jesus
First Disciples
Woman at the Well
Jesus at Nazareth and Capernaum
Jesus and the Lepers
Thirty Pieces of Silver
Upper Room, The
Betrayal in Gethsemane
Jesus Before the High Priest
Trial Before Pilate
Lord is Risen, The
Lord's Ascension, The
Birth of John the Baptist
Ministry of John the Baptist
Jesus and the Fishermen
Thy Sins Are Forgiven
Jesus, Lord of the Sabbath
Transfiguration, The
Jesus Teaches Forgiveness
Before Abraham Was, I Am
Jesus Heals the Man Born Blind
I Am the Resurrection
Last Journey to Jerusalem
Crucifixion, The
Nicodemus

NUDE FILMOGRAPHY

Filming dates and by whom are unknown, but probably were filmed from the late 1940s to the late 1950s.

Annie From Montana
Babes in Woods
Balloon Busted!
Eve's Pleasure
February Second Week
Girls on the Loose
Macau
Nude Dude

Scenes from "Nude Dude" on the western street set

NUDE PHOTOSHOOTS

A popular pastime for photographers was the nude photoshoot. The photos in this section are from the 1940s to 1950s plus a few from 2011.

Garden of the Gods

Garden of the Gods area

276

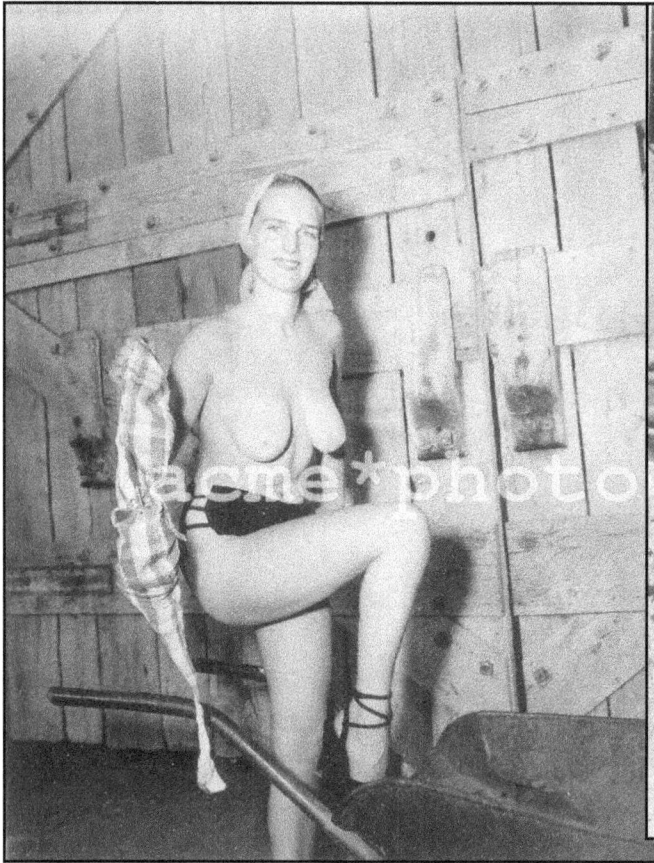

HISTORIC DRIVING DIRECTIONS

From Los Angeles, the Iverson Movie Ranch was located about 31 miles northwest, at the far northwestern end of the San Fernando Valley. Once you reached the San Fernando Valley, there were two main routes east/west: state route 118 along Devonshire Blvd. on the northern side of the valley and state route 101 along Ventura Blvd. on the southern side of the valley. On the western end of the valley was Topanga Canyon Blvd (state route 27) when ran north/south. At the northern end of route 27, where it connected with route 118, Santa Susana Pass Road began and which road headed north for a short ways before turning westerly. After passing over the train tunnel, in about a half mile or so, you came to an unmarked dirt road on the right/north side of the road. That was the entrance to the Iverson Movie Ranch. If you followed that road to its end, you would be at the main ranch house area of the ranch.

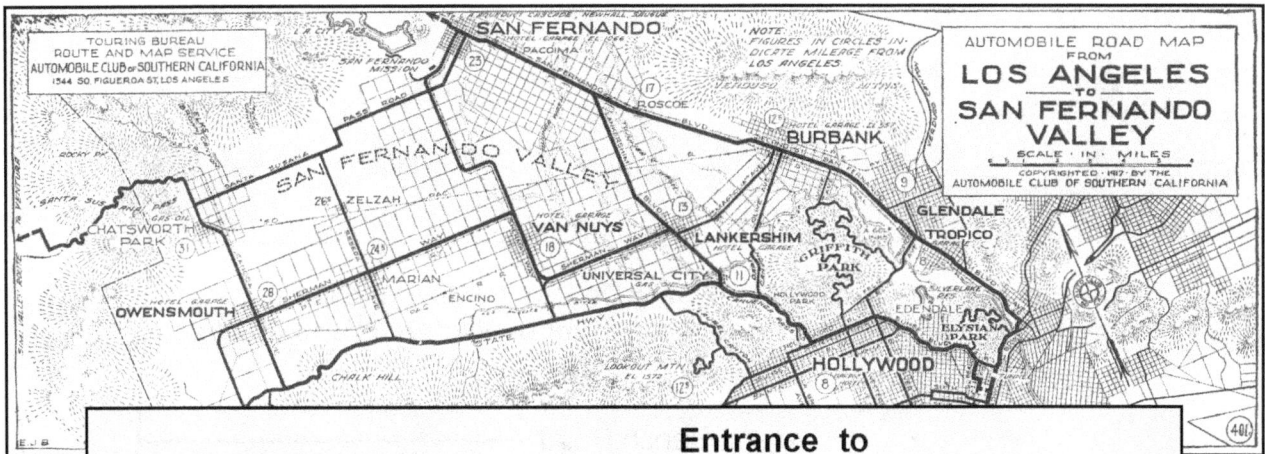

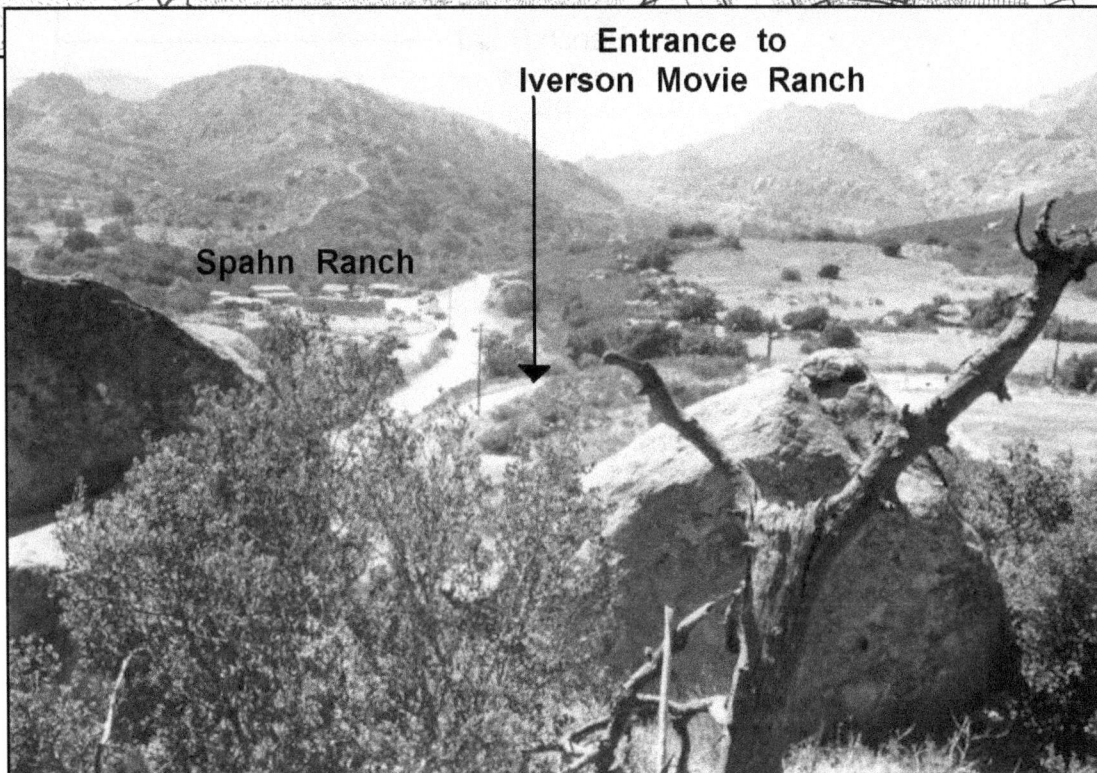

Entrance to Iverson Movie Ranch

Spahn Ranch

283

Scene from a sequence filmed for **Flying Deuces** (1939) but not used.
Became stock footage which was used in **Manhunt of Mystery Island** (1945).

Iverson Ranch Road ——————————————
Railroad Tunnel ——————————————
Santa Susana Pass Road ——————————————